Experimental Stitchery

Arline K. Morrison currently teaches at the Cambridge Center for Adult Education in Cambridge, Massachusetts. Her fiber art is represented in many private collections, and has been exhibited in several gallerys and museums in New England.

ARLINE K. MORRISON

Experimental
Stitchery

AND

OTHER FIBER TECHNIQUES

A SPECTRUM BOOK

PRENTICE-HALL, INC., Englewood Cliffs, New Jersey 07632

Library of Congress Cataloging in Publication Data

Morrison, Arline K
    Experimental stitchery and other fiber techniques.

    (The Creative handcrafts series) (A Spectrum Book)
    Bibliography: p.
    Includes index.
    1. Textile crafts. I. Title.
TT699.M68   746   76-26015
ISBN 0-13-295050-8
ISBN 0-13-295048-0 pbk.

Frontispiece: *Three Forms*
(Arline K. Morrison. Photograph by Paul Brandford;
courtesy of Little, Brown and Company).

© 1977 by Prentice-Hall, Inc.
Englewood Cliffs, New Jersey 07632

A SPECTRUM BOOK

10 9 8 7 6 5 4 3 2 1

Printed in the United States of America

Prentice-Hall International, Inc., *London*
Prentice-Hall of Australia Pty. Limited, *Sydney*
Prentice-Hall of Canada, Ltd., *Toronto*
Prentice-Hall of India Private Limited, *New Delhi*
Prentice-Hall of Japan, Inc., *Tokyo*
Prentice-Hall of Southeast Asia Pte. Ltd., *Singapore*
Whitehall Books Limited, *Wellington, New Zealand*

In memory of Patric Dion Morrison,
whose love and keen observance of the natural world
is a continuing inspiration in my life.

Contents

Acknowledgments

When undertaking a project such as this book, one is grateful for the many helpful ways in which others lighten the task. I should like to thank the following individuals for their contributions toward creating this book:

Elizabeth Bole Eddison and Alice Sizer Warner of Warner-Eddison Associates, Inc., for their encouragement, useful suggestions, and the use of the company typewriter

Robert Williams, Jr., manager of The Camera Place, for his generosity in the loan of photographic equipment

Christopher Morrison, who is responsible for all of the photographs (unless otherwise noted), for a difficult job well and cheerfully done

The artists who so generously allowed their work to be photographed for use in the book

And Michael Morrison, for guidance, continuous encouragement, and moral support.

1 Introduction

What makes stitchery different from needlework? Beginning students in stitchery classes, many of whom are experienced in the needle arts, are confused when they are told that needlework and stitchery are quite different even though the same process in forming stitches is used for each. The answer is simple and straightforward: needlework is an end in itself, that end being a correct, perfectly formed stitch. Stitchery, on the other hand, is only a means to an end, that end being an idea, a concept, or a statement worked in fiber with the stitches manipulated in any way one can conceive to achieve the desired result.

Stitchery now appears on the walls of industrial and municipal buildings, institutions, museums, and galleries, as well as in private homes. It has come into its own as a recognized art form. Much credit for the ascent of stitchery and related fiber arts to this level should go to Mariska Karasz who, in the 1950s, brought the art to the attention of the public which until then had not fully realized the potential of this medium for the creation of strong art statements. Twenty years later, there is still a long way to go toward public awareness of the power of fiber art. Ms. Karasz' work, unorthodox in both use of materials and in interpretation, is simple, strong, and vibrant. It has excited the imagination of many artists, many of them originally painters, and

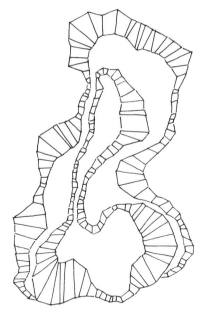

Fig. 1.1 Meandering stitch.

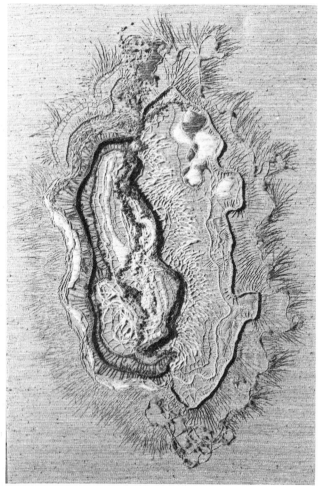

Fig. 1.2 *The Long March* (author).

prompted some of them to explore the satisfying medium of fiber in the pursuit of their art. Many of Mariska Karasz' pieces are in permanent museum collections. Her hanging, "Calla Lily," is in the collection of Cooper-Hewitt Museum of Decorative Arts and Design, Smithsonian Institution.

One of the most difficult hurdles to overcome for many stitchery students, especially those experienced in embroidery and sewing, is to accept the concept of freedom to deviate from the established form of a stitch. It seems almost anarchic to them when it is suggested. A good way to overcome this barrier is to take a very ordinary stitch, for instance a squared chain, and start a line of it on a cloth backing. It will be noticed by the stitcher that the simplest and most uncomplicated of stitches are frequently most amenable to manipulation and distortion. Begin your line of chaining away from the edge somewhere near the middle of your backing. Meander with it, as if it were a path through a wood, widening it, compressing it, making it very dense and compact, then, by contrast, spreading it out widely and freely. Notice the variation in shapes and spaces resulting from this distortion. Envision your woodland path through the forest, the trail sometimes narrow and insignificant then emerging into a clearing with space to stride out with no constraint. Your trail should be twisting, turning, often to the point of going back on itself. When one line of stitching is finished, study it, noting the difference in spatial relationships, and the linear aspect of your path. Then repeat the process with another line of stitching adjacent to the first, sometimes running parallel with the first line, sometimes diverging from it, then once again converging (see Fig.1.1).

When engaging in this exercise, one is struck by the possibilities of design in the age-old stitches done by needlepeople for the last few hundred years, and by the spontaneity and contemporary look of what one has just done. It's like opening a door to a whole new world of expression and the joy of this revelation is immeasurable.

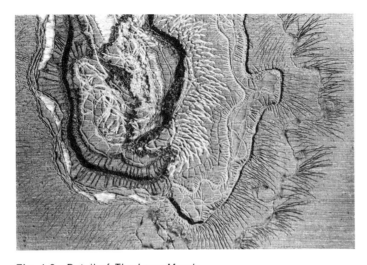

Fig. 1.3 Detail of *The Long March*.

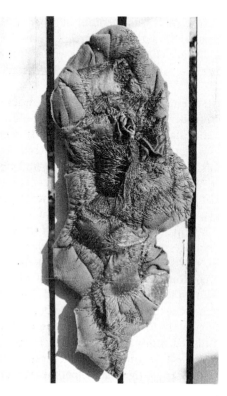

Fig. 1.4 *Renaissance*—stuffed with appliqué and stitchery (author).

Fig. 1.5 Detail of *Renaissance*.

"I'm not a bit creative, but I like to sew. . . ."

"I can't design, but I do know a lot of stitches. . . ."

"I'm really very traditional, but I'd like to try a more spontaneous and modern approach. . . ."

These comments are typical in an experimental stitchery class during the early sessions. It is important for everyone to realize that we are all creative to one degree or another, in one area or another. A positive attitude is a plus factor to bring to an experimental stitchery class or to working on one's own. The warmth of fiber, its interesting tactile qualities, and seemingly endless color variations are challenging to the imagination if handling and working with fiber are pleasing. Process rather than result is the most significant factor in experimental stitchery, as well as in many aspects of life itself. "The joy of life lies in the doing, not in the done." It is sometimes hard for students to unburden themselves of the preoccupation with result; as a consequence, they are reluctant to experiment, to try out an idea which seems pretty far out.

One comes to realize that the purpose of the experimental approach to stitchery is innovation—to continually ask oneself "what if . . . ?" and then pursue the line of thought in one's work—never mind the result. You cannot make a "mistake" because there is no one "right" approach. The way to

4

accomplish pleasing, exciting results, is always to dare to try what you have not yet done. Once you have mastered a certain approach, don't keep grinding it out just because you do it well and gain admiration for your pieces. You will just become a hack and retard your growth as an artist. Some of your experiments will be worth preserving; others will not. Whatever the end result is, you will have learned something—if only what *not* to do! One should go beyond asking "why?" to saying "why not? . . ." Risk is part of every experiment; through risk you become vulnerable to failure and nonrecognition, but in the long range your work will be better and you will have learned valuable lessons not only about art but about life. "The things which hurt, instruct." (Some of my own less-than-successful experiments have wound up as an addition to the local goodwill box, along with the more practical clothing and household goods. I feel they might be good for a laugh and enliven someone's day.) It is good to be able to laugh at one's own work and not be too ego-wounded by the failures.

One very useful tool for any designer/craftsperson is the keeping of a notebook for recording project ideas, color, design and technique notes, sketches, clippings, and the like. More than just an adjunct to your study of stitchery and other fiber methods, it can be a reflection of all the components which make up the whole person—you—if it is kept with thoughtfulness, introspection, sensitivity, and conscientiousness. This was made evident to me when the keeping of a notebook was part of the curriculum of a dynamic design class taught by Mary Ventre, author of *Crochet*, and an accomplished fiber artist. Because of the positive personal value gained from this assignment, I have since made a similar recommendation to my students, although it is not a requirement.

In a design notebook, all sorts of things are grist for your mill: lines of poetry, quotations, philosophical concepts, photographs, drawings, reproductions of paintings, advertisements, pages of your own sketches, plans, doodles (sometimes the subliminal-like doodling reveals potential for beautiful designs . . .), pressed leaves, flowers, small root systems. All facets of life are sources of inspiration that give the artist a storehouse of ideas to draw upon when searching for the germination of a project. Anyone looking through your notebook should have a pretty accurate picture of what kind of person you are. In a class, it is often a good idea to urge that each student start a notebook at the beginning of the session. Then, near the end of the term, all students are asked to bring their books to class for other students to look over. In many classes the groups tend to be rather small and intimate; the conversation sometimes veers from the subject at hand while people are working and they get to know one another quite well after a few weeks. When the notebooks are passed around their contents frequently reveal much more about each person than had been gleaned from the class meetings, and appreciation for the complexity of one's fellows is enhanced. Sometimes the notebooks one keeps are so intimate and introspective as to be painfully private and one is reluctant to bare one's soul by showing the contents to colleagues. This, of course, should be respected. The purpose of these experimental stitchery classes is self-fulfillment and to experience the joy which springs

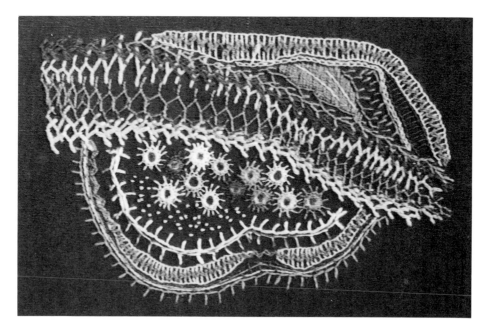

Fig. 1.6 *Sagittarius Rising* (Martha Liller).

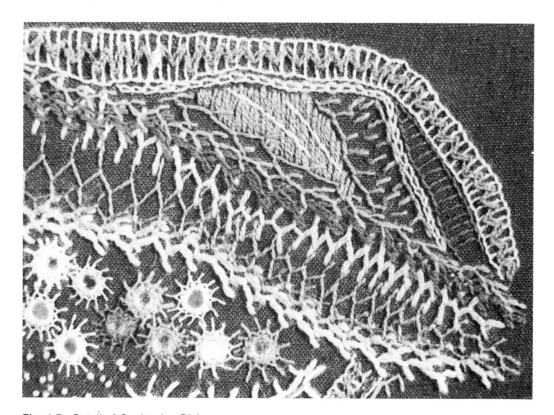

Fig. 1.7 Detail of *Sagittarius Rising.*

from the process of creation. Consequently, flexibility is encouraged and no one is obliged to do anything which would jeopardize inner privacy. Some students resist the idea of notebooks for this reason, and others simply because they don't want to bother with them. In spite of these reactions, though, I am convinced of the worth of a well-kept notebook and the idea is broached to each new group of students.

The world around us goes largely unobserved by many people who are so preoccupied by the pressures of everyday living that their powers of observation have been numbed and stultified. When engaging in any artistic endeavor, regardless of your chosen medium, learn to sharpen your powers of *seeing* the world around you, not just looking at it superficially. The hues of winter and those of winter fading into spring, the tender young colors of emerging spring—all the seasons with their beginning, middle, and ending periods have a distinct coloration which deserves to be noticed and seldom is, except for autumn whose flamboyance is hard to ignore even by the most jaded. Although autumn foliage tours and pilgrimages to upcountry New England are a big thing, it's too bad that the other seasons with their more subtle beauty are most often passed over.

If you really give thought to *seeing* you world, your spirit will be enriched by so many sights previously unnoticed: the patterns of cast shadows, the tracery of foliage against the sky, the lacy etching of skeletal tree branches, the gentle curve of grasses with their nodding seed heads, the filaments of spiders' webs, sometimes dew-spangled, the muted tones of stones and shells. The shapes, textures, curves, and designs of a myriad of things in the natural world will excite your imagination and provide inspiration for your work.

Similarly, man-made world should not be neglected in your efforts toward heightened awareness. Buildings, fences, brick, metal, glass, humble implements of daily living; the forms, shapes, and patterns of objects in juxtaposition with one another; the negative spaces resulting from groupings—should be looked at thoughtfully, evaluated, pondered. An excellent book called *Forms in Japan*, by Yuichiro Kojiro, deals with the beauty in utilitarian objects necessary for ordinary living—rakes, forks, baskets, wrappings, utensils, combs, all sorts of implements we use all the time and never *see*. The Scandinavian designers also have a reverence for everyday objects and feel that everyone is entitled to good design in the things we need and use daily—that excellence in design should not be relegated to the fortunate few. Their philosophy toward the day-to-day products of living is embodied in the slogan, "More beautiful things for everyday use"; they feel that the function of a designer is "to give each individual the possibility of a purposeful and happy life." Beautiful, spare, gracefully designed objects are the hallmark of Scandinavian design.

A good exercise to increase awareness is to choose an object, natural or man-made, and make a series of sketches showing all aspects of that object: its color, shape, and texture; its qualities of lightness or heaviness, transparency or density; its strength; its delicacy. Explore in your sketches as much as you can of the very essence of that object. Repeat this with other things. Study your results; by the time you finish, you should really *know* that

Fig. 1.8 Dried bittersweet root system; note intricate linear pattern of the roots—an inspiration for design.

Fig. 1.9 Driftwood—a natural sculpture.

Fig. 1.10 Rock forms and sand patterns—design inspiration.

Fig. 1.11 Rock textures and forms; note sensuous quality of rock formation in foreground.

Fig. 1.12 Dried sunflower heads.

object. Begin collecting things which excite you, both natural and man made. Stones, twigs, bark, lichens, dry seed heads, grasses, root systems, dry sea weeds, shells, wasp and bird nests, feathers, interesting rusted bits of metal (these are lovely used with needle-lace), beach glass—all these things are only a minute list of possibilities for a collection. Observe these things carefully. Look at the patterns, the striations, the textures, color, structure, and shape. Examine them through a magnifying glass and make more sketches of what you see. Make color swatches of seasonal and midseasonal color schemes. All of these exercises will sharpen your powers of observation and pique your imagination which will, in turn, help in your stitchery. The transition from wanting to make something to getting an idea for a design will be much easier if you have a storehouse of observations in your mental filing cabinet. In addition, your appreciation of the world around you will be increased greatly by all the things you are now really *seeing*. Consider some of your collection pieces as possible art forms to display in your house.

Last summer, we grew a few very handsome sun flowers in the vegetable garden, both as a decorative touch and for bird food. When the flowers, having bloomed and their seeds having provided a bird feast, began to wither, we let them dry completely in the garden, not digging them out. They evolved into very interesting studies in rich earth colors, beiges, umber, yellow-ochre. The shapes of the dried, twisted petals, the curved stems, the center, now empty of seeds, were fascinating to study (see Fig. 1.12). They are now arranged in an old crock which sits on a bookcase in the living room where they can be seen and provide a continual source of inspiration. They are excellent subjects for sketches, which of course, can be translated into stitcheries. However, the top of the stalk was not the only part of the sunflower to become a subject for study. When the garden was turned over in fall, the remaining sunflower stalk was uprooted and discarded. Before it became an official part of the compost pile, I cut off the root system (see Fig. 1.13) with about twelve inches of stalk, and let the whole thing dry thoroughly. It was really lovely, the heavier roots contrasting with those finer and more threadlike. The lacelike appearance of these fibers was especially noticeable when held against a background; the interesting way in which the stalk emerged from this complex tangle of roots added to the sculptural composition. It now hangs on a wall and holds its own as an art form. All the design elements and lessons one could wish to learn exist in the natural world. Develop your eyes to truly *see.*

The world of fiber has, of course, never been the exclusive province of women. Both men and women have achieved strong statements in various aspects of stitchery and related textile arts. Nik Krevitsky's* stitcheries are stimulating to those who want to use an abstract approach in their work. Mr.

*Author of *Stitchery, Art and Craft.*

Fig. 1.13 Root system of sunflower plant; note design possibilities in this natural structure.

Krevitsky works with a minimum number of different stitches, concentrating on use of transparent and translucent gauzes, organdies, nettings, and similar materials as well as opaque fabrics, superimposed on each other to accomplish unusual colorplay appropriate to the concept and mood he is working to express. The simplicity of his stitches, sometimes just a straight stitch, is extremely effective in the linear and textural results he gets. A good example of his technique is *Landscape: Flower Garden*, which appears on the cover of his book, *Stitchery, Art and Craft*.

Norman Laliberte,* a distinguished banner-maker, works with very brilliant colors, especially suitable for banners, and does his stitching mostly by machine. His work is bold, exuberant, and eye-stopping; his figures are very stylized and the whole effect has strong visual impact.

Walter Nottingham's works are large, very sculptural, and done mainly in crochet and other similar means of yarn manipulation. *Celibacy*, one of his more familiar works which is often reproduced in fiber art books, is a large (108″ X 36″) wall-piece done mostly in a variety of shades of red with black accents. Its many small crocheted component cylindrical parts are attached to an oval shape in high relief, with tendrils of yarns hanging from that shape. It is an eloquent and powerful piece. One of his works, *Maine Shore*, which is a personal favorite, was part of a show a few years ago at De Cordova Museum in Lincoln, Massachusetts. It is an arrangement of forms suggesting marine life, seaweeds, rocks, all reminiscent of a tidal pool. It was done in the muted greens, ochres, and browns appropriate to the subject and lay upon a platform about a foot or so off the ground floor. I have never forgotten that piece.

There are many men in the field doing exciting things—I've mentioned only a few. But in spite of this, the myth persists that stitchery and the related textile arts are for females only. It would be desirable if this attitude would perish and if more men would begin to work with some of the fiber techniques in a serious way. It seems a pity that a potentially satisfying means of expression is now pursued mainly by women.

I considered it a breakthrough when, in 1974, I had my first male student, who not only was very quick to grasp the idea of experimentation in fiber, but who was completely unself-conscious as a lone male among females. He contributed much to the class as a student and if he should decide to continue his fiber work he would be capable of doing some very interesting and pleasing pieces. I hope the enrollment of the first male student in my class presages a new, enlightened trend. Maybe the publication of Roosevelt (''Rosey'') Grier's book on needlepoint will help tear down barriers which never should have existed in the first place!

In stitchery and the other textile arts, many pieces are designed and executed with a concept as inspiration. Love, death, war, peace, politics, society, justice, equality, protest, freedom—all the ideas which are important to human beings have generated the creative imaginings of artists and have provoked valid and powerful artistic statements.

*Author of *Banners and Hangings: Design and Construction*.

Fig. 1.14 *The Bombing of Bach Mai Hospital* (author).

It is important to try to know oneself as much as one ever can, beclouded as most of us are by ego, self-deception, and subjective rather than objective judgment. Examine your personal attitudes toward life, the ideas that seem important to you: what makes you happy, tranquil, excited, melancholy, miserable, angry, depressed, agonized. Choose some one of these attitudes or a concept or an idea—something intangible—that is stimulating to your imagination. Think of the colors which seem best to suggest that intangible something; i.e., red—excitement, anger, aggressiveness, boldness, vitality; blue—serenity, tranquillity, coolness, self-control. Then choose the yarns and fabric which seem similarly appropriate to carry out the theme. Is it tender, delicate, sensitive, ethereal? Is it bold, massive, angry, demanding? Is it controlled, self-disciplined, quiet, serene, calm? Whatever attitude or idea you have in mind, gather together materials relevant to express your concept. Then start your stitching. Some artists prefer to begin directly, letting the design grow as each new element is added. Others prefer to make a series of sketches, planning the projected finished result with more deliberation. This is a matter of personal decision. The stitches chosen should reflect, too, the qualities which prompted your choice of materials. Doing several pieces from an intangible idea is an excellent way in which to practice self-examination. Sometimes facets of one's character are revealed which one might prefer had been left undiscovered. But it is reasonable to suppose that in the long run, you will advance as an artist and grow as a person through these discoveries even though some mental anguish might be encountered during this growth period.

In the succeeding chapters of this book, many areas of stitchery and fiber arts will be discussed and a list of recommended books will be provided for those who wish to delve deeper into the world of fiber (see the Bibliography). We will talk about methods of developing an idea and then beginning a project, suggest materials and tools, and explain how to mix several textile techniques harmoniously in one piece and how to create soft sculpture and relief. You will also find many design exercises to stimulate your imagination, instructions for special techniques with which you may be unfamiliar, and other practical information to make your experience less rocky as you start your experimentation.

Let's begin!

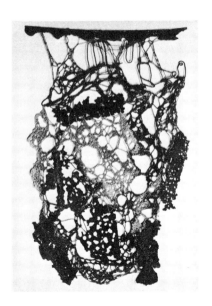

2 Materials

In today's world of fiber art, there are no boundaries surrounding the kinds of materials being used by imaginative artists in their search for ways and means of self-expression. Indeed, materials go beyond fibers in many instances. Wire, plastic tubing, rubber bands, twigs, bark, buttons, beads, fur, string, rope—all these and many other seemingly more bizarre items join the familiar yarns, threads, roving, unspun wool, and fabrics to bring to the experimental fiber artist an assortment of materials which give wide scope to the rendering of ideas.

When planning a piece and selecting materials with which to interpret an idea, it is important to analyze the properties of each material in question. Consider what can be achieved with whatever you are using; its innate qualities will determine the limits to what you can do with it. Obviously, it is futile to expect to stitch with a thick and thin yarn on a tightly woven cloth used as a backing or working surface. The yarn cannot be drawn through the fabric. That type of yarn would be very effective used in couching (couching is simply sewing down one yarn with another which is more readily amenable to being drawn in and out of a backing), or in crocheting, either directly on the backing or as a separate element which you will attach later. When selecting your yarns for a project, decide also on the method planned and choose

15

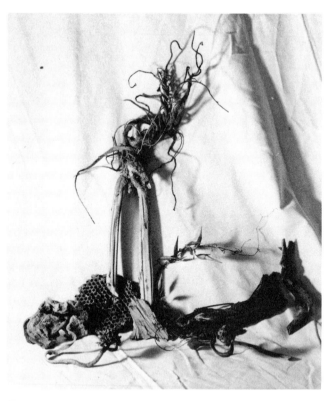

Fig. 2.1 Construction of rope, yarn, rusted bits of hardware, old rubber hose, and wire (author).

Fig. 2.2 Natural objects suitable for fiber statements. Consider inclusion of found objects in fiber designs.

accordingly. Much irritation and frustration can be avoided by thinking ahead. Sometimes yarns are just moderately difficult to work with. They fray or break easily, they snarl, they are somewhat uneven in texture. If the effect accomplished by using them is sufficiently interesting, it is sometimes worth the small struggle involved. But try to avoid unnecessary difficulties in the actual working process—there are enough design problems to contend with without additional aggravation thrown in! A realistic attitude toward the things you work with will help considerably toward making the creative process fulfilling and joyful.

The kinds of cloth one can elect to use as a backing (working surface) are many and varied, and what is chosen should reflect the mood of the proposed design idea. Loosely woven fabrics such as burlap, monk's cloth, homespun, and similar types of casual "country-look" materials are very easy to work with, even with heavy yarns, because of their loose weave. If you wish a more formally elegant appearance to the design you might choose velvet, velveteen, plushy unwaled corduroy, satins, or raw silk. Heavy linen is very nice to work on, as is wool. The selection is large as you will discover when browsing in fabric stores. Upholstery shops, too, sometimes sell remnants of very intriguing materials suitable for stitcheries.

The unusual materials being seen in today's fiber art excite the senses and stimulate the imagination to consider the as yet untried in one's pieces. I remember one very expressive and graceful hanging shown in an exhibit at the Museum of Fine Arts School in Boston made entirely of knotted rubber bands forming a network of open spaces, the spatial relationships varying because of the elasticity of the rubber bands working in conjunction with gravity as the work hung in slightly diagonal soft folds on the wall. One really forgot that these were humble rubber bands; this was a good example of a material transcending its origins to astonish the viewer by its new identity.

Parachute cord is lovely to work with. It knots and braids beautifully, and can be couched down to develop an interesting silky-looking texture. It can often be obtained at Army and Navy stores and is well worth buying if you encounter it.

Electronic hookup wire, the thin, plastic insulated wire used in the electronics industry, is very satisfying to experiment with. If you know someone working in an electronics plant where this wire is used, plead for some odds and ends. The colors of the coating on the wires are gay and appear in rather unusual combinations. When braided or combined with yarns, they make exciting adjuncts to hangings or soft sculpture. They can also be used independently, in developing forms. A very pleasing piece, using this wire, was done by a member of a design class who made a three-dimensional open ball-shaped form. The work was designed to be ceiling hung and the artist developed the shape by braiding the wires, using those braids to form the sphere. In the next chapter I will describe, along with other methods, simple braiding, and also braiding with braids.

Ordinary strings, twines, and ropes are excellent things to manipulate. Look in your supermarket, stationery store, and hardware store for strings of many kinds. Yellow mason's twine is a tight twisted cord in a lovely soft yellow color and which responds nicely to many procedures. I've used it in simple knotting, braiding, coiling (a basketry method, discussed in Chapter 10), off-loom weaving, crocheting, couching, and in soft sculpture. It assumes a shape quickly and needs no support, being firm and lively.

Jute is another pleasing twine and seems to be very much in favor among artists currently working in fiber. It comes in a wide variety of hues as well as its own natural color, and in various thicknesses. It, too, is very firm when worked in crochet, knotting, or braiding. It ravels nicely and interesting effects can be obtained by undoing the plies and freeing the individual fibers.

Sisal is rather hard to handle but gives a satisfying result when worked up. It is less malleable than some of the other twines and is very springy as well as being hard on the hands. However, the same positive aspects mentioned in connection with jute apply to sisal. The light creamy color is particularly pleasant.

Similar in many respects to sisal is baling twine which I found in a farm supply store. It came in a very large ball and is a muted apricot color. The color alone, which is rather unusual, was sufficient incentive to add it to my materials collection. It was also very inexpensive.

Designing with String by Mary Seyd is a good source of ideas if one wishes to delve more deeply into strings and twines as a medium of expression.

Flexible plastic tubing is fun to use, especially when combined with yarns, wire or other materials. One can easily manipulate the tubing to make a bold version of needle-lace. (How to make free unstructured needle-lace is explained in Chapter 10.) Creating an offbeat and unlikely version of the more usual delicate and ephemeral result one gets when using this technique provides a jolt to the senses. Other plastics are equally provocative to use. Bread wrappers, plastic wrap, and bags can be crumpled, twisted ropelike, spread flat and sewn upon, crocheted—if you have a large quantity—or simply attached as a component part of a design. A hanging of mine made several years ago has a piece of twisted plastic bag couched down next to a large rough-textured appliquéd area and in that design it works. Firm plastic, either transparent or opaque, can readily become an element of your stitchery

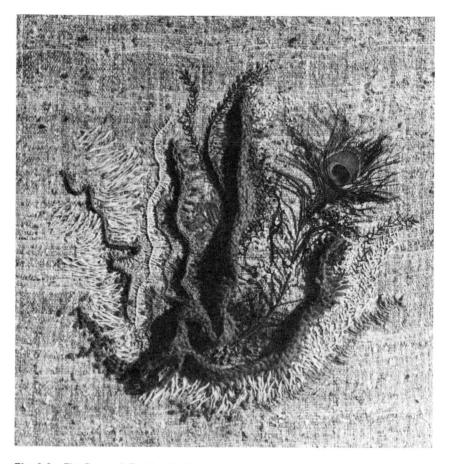

Fig. 2.3 *The Peacock Feather* (author).

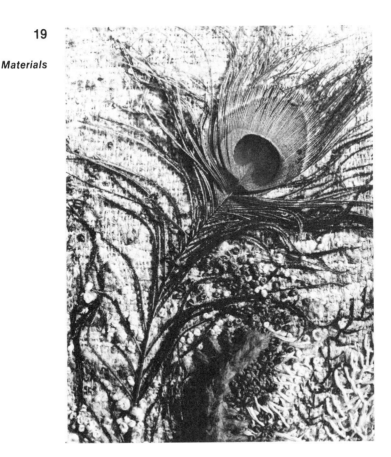

Fig. 2.4   Detail of *The Peacock Feather*.

designs. In the piece just mentioned, the design also included two large sections in which the fabric was cut away and two pieces of firm transparent plastic were sewn in the negative spaces. The design is very spare and the use of plastic seemed to express the mood properly.

In your search for yarns you will discover that the outlets catering to weavers offer the most exciting wares. You will find all sorts of colors, fibers, textures, and mixtures. Rough, thick, hand-spun yarns, with some bits of dried plant debris still clinging to them, silky-smooth yarns and threads with colors almost unbearably beautiful, blends of colors, nubbly thicks and thins, soft-as-a-cloud mohair—they all spill out of their bins to beguile and enchant the purchaser. The selection is seemingly endless, with new things continually appearing. A velvety yarn called chinchilla was sent to me recently from Germany. This version has long fibers on a base thread. I had seen its shorter-fibered cousin in our local stores, but the long-haired variety was new to me.

There is also a velvet yarn (expensive) in rich stained-glass colors. I hesitate to use the term "yarn" to describe these fibers, and thread seems to connote something thin which these are not, but it appears reasonable and practical to group everything fibrous coming in a ball or a hank under the general category of "yarns."

I caution anyone going into a shop that carries all these fascinating things to buy cautiously and sparingly. It is only too easy to get carried away and overspend. For stitchery—unlike weaving—you don't need huge quantities of a yarn; you need small amounts of a variety of yarns. Most places have a winding machine and will wind off from the large cone a ball of whatever size you wish, weighing the ball and selling it for so much an ounce. This way you can get a wide selection of different things without going bankrupt.

In your delight at all the lovely man-made yarns, threads, textiles, and other supplies don't neglect the natural world and its bounty. A walk along the street will sometimes yield many potentially useful things—fallen pine cones, nuts (opened nut shells have intriguing patterns), leaves, pine needles, twigs, pieces of bark, and seed pods. As suggested in Chapter 1, start your collection and use these things in your work. Some of my best hanging rods for wall pieces are branches found during casual walks and errands.

The curving twisting branches of bittersweet, the shrub which clambers in dense tangles along New England roadsides, are excellent to use in stitcheries. On several occasions I've sewn a branch directly on a backing, using it as a starting point for a design. The twigs are strong, not easily broken, sometimes almost curly in their configuration. They can be left untouched when attached to the backing, providing linear interest. Because they stand out from the working surface, the cast shadows from them are an additional design factor. It is also interesting to wrap them completely with yarn or wire and (or) to needle-weave from branch to base surface, making your design three-dimensional. Bittersweet is very easily grown if you live in a climate compatible to the plant. The branches and berries are so attractive, as well as being of practical use to the artist, it is worth trying to start a plant if you have the space. One autumn I put cut branches of the berries in our flower boxes. The following year we had several small plants starting in the garden where the berries had fallen off and seeded themselves; the vines are now growing vigorously up the front of the house and over the roof almost to the ridgepole. So it *is* easy to grow! And you will have your own personal supply to use in your work.

Similarly, in beach strolls and in the woods pick up the dried plant life, lichens, mosses, shells, twisted roots, weathered driftwood, bits of beach glass, and lavendar wampum (the shells the Indians used for money); all these things may, in their turn, prove to be just the right touch for one of your designs.

A collection I made of beach glass wound up on a piece which was designed for an ocean-front house. The piece was done in needlelace technique using fine copper-, brass-, and silver-colored wires intermingled with bits of amber and moss green beach glass worked into the "lace." The whole thing was attached to a large, wire-wrapped oval frame and hung in a window where the light coming through the glass was the right touch to provide a focus for the design. So you never know . . . .

It is very satisfying to be able to transform reused things into new and vital forms. Recycling has become an issue in our lives and experimental stitchery and other fiber methods offer ample opportunity to exercise one's inventiveness in devising ways to recycle when designing one's works. In a piece done several years ago, which combined knitting and stitchery done on top of the knitted surface, it was necessary to have the bottom weighted to give proper tension to the knitted backing. In searching the cellar workbench with its house-repair flotsam and jetsam, I found a box of fishing sinkers which were perfect for my weighting problem.

The kitchen cupboard was the source for a material which worked out effectively on a wall hanging. The brown homespun backing of the piece was partially covered by a copper pot scrubber, which had been taken apart, flattened, and spread out over a section of the brown background. Stitchery was then done on both the fabric and the metallic mesh in harmonious colors to complement the copper and brown. Pot scrubber mesh is very attractive and its use is yet another example of using the familiar in unfamiliar ways.

In a large hanging by Debby Gressel, shown in a 1975 exhibition at City Hall in Boston, Massachusetts, hundreds of white plastic concave discs about 1 inch in diameter—originally packing material—were strung together in long vertical strands. The theme of the hanging was man's exploration in space; some of the discs were broken to create texture, others were left intact. It was an innovative and sensitive use of materials—and also recycled that which had already served its initial function.

The small pull-tabs from soft drink cans have also been grouped effectively on hangings. One should train the eye and mind to perceive the qualities in objects which lend themselves to new uses, regardless of their origins and past history.

Of particular interest to me are the bits of rusted corroded metal I often find in the street or on the sidewalk. The corrosion sometimes causes a lacelike effect which, when combined with needle-lace, produces hangings of great charm (see Fig. 2.5). The two seemingly incompatible elements complement each other in a surprisingly harmonious way. These metal fragments are often so fatigued that one must handle them with a good deal of care because of their fragility and brittleness. Their weathered colors can be subtle and very handsome.

The need for economy can stir one to new heights of innovation and sensitivity regarding the use of old things or discards. Don't throw away the outdated tattered clothing before scanning it carefully for anything you might be able to use in the future—the buttons, the zippers, the trimmings, or the useable portions of the cloth itself. The strings of beads you are tired of, the rusty nuts and bolts, the curiously shaped pieces of wood and metal, snippets of leather, Aunt Lavinia's moth-eaten fur—all these and many more are possibilities for transformed function in art statements.

Many contemporary craftspeople make very handsome jewelry from unlikely oddments. When they were small, my boys took an old alarm clock apart and methodically hammered flat several of the large clock pieces. Once having reduced the clock to rubble they lost interest in it. The shapes they

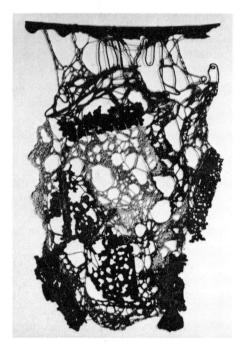

Fig. 2.5 Needle-lace hanging with bits of corroded rusty metal in the lace (author).

pounded out were quite nice so I rescued the remains and put them in my pile of possibles for future use. Pieces of that clock eventually attained new status as a necklace with the metal parts serving as a focal point for asymmetrical knotting done in ashy rose and yellow ochre carpet thread, the knotting pulling all the separate elements together in a unified entity. The necklace is unusual, fun to wear, and was interesting to make.

A wall-piece which was challenging to create was initially begun using a broken brake disk from a VW as a nucleous (see Fig. 2.8). The resulting hanging with its scraps of metal shavings (rescued from a machine shop trash can) and yarn-wrapped old rope often provokes amusing—and amused—comments from visitors. Another similar piece was made with a rusty piece of VW innards—part of a muffler, I think—that I found lying in our driveway. Keeping the VW entrails as the focal center of interest, I used braided rough-textured yarns in rust, dull mustard, and soft browns to augment the metal. It now hangs in someone's house and it too causes some curious observations among its viewers.

Part of the value in working in fiber arts is the continual heightened awareness to one's world which develops in the artist. Do not feel that you must always have brand-new bright and beautiful materials to work with before you can express yourself. Meaningful works are often generated from the mundane throwaway. Learn to evaluate things in their current state of being and forget original function. I once saw an old wooden toilet seat used in juxtaposition with weaving in a handsome and elegant wall hanging. The natural wood of the seat, the oval shape with its negative space, was perfectly integrated with the woven area, resulting in a design success. It was an excellent

Fig. 2.6 Knotted yarn hanging with brass Indian bells and recycled guitar strings (author).

Fig. 2.7 Hanging using sisal, rough-textured yarns, and bamboo beads on natural burlap (author).

Fig. 2.8 Hanging using rough-textured yarns, rope, industrial waste (metal shavings), and a VW brake disk (author).

illustration of an artist looking at this old abandoned seat with only the shape, line, color, and texture in mind.

During the social upheavals of recent years many strong statements have been made by fiber artists to express their views on the issues confronting the world. War, civil rights, justice and injustice, economics, rights of women, starvation, ecology, politics, corruption—all these realities have stirred artists, whatever their medium, to speak out, to protest, to agonize, to communicate their feelings through their art. Some years ago, I saw a hanging which made a lasting impression on me. Called *Tree, Vietnam, Cambodia,* done by Ruth Springer of Maine, it was a ceiling-hung weaving. The yarns used were dark, brooding shades in somber khaki, olive, green, and black, descending in long, uneven shades from a piece of barbed wire. It was a simple, stark statement which conveyed without equivocation the horror in Southeast Asia. The opportunities for concerned artists to contribute their talents in the struggle for a better world are there for those whose interests lie in these directions. Ms. Springer's use of barbed wire from which to hang her weaving, combined with the funeral hues of her yarns, symbolized her message eloquently.

There are, of course, pitfalls in using any materials. No matter what you use it is very easy to overdo just as a painter can overpaint. One can become so enamored of the material that too much is done with it thus cheapening the end result. It is especially easy to do this when using metallic threads, sequins, and other flashy things. Unless you deliberately want to make a statement that demands the use of theatrical and flamboyant material, beware of it. A very telling wall hanging, done by Sally Oliver, and shown at the Boston City Hall exhibit mentioned before, was called *The Combat Zone* (Boston's name for its "adult" entertainment district). Among the materials used on this piece were strident purple velvet, feathers, sequins, and silky fringe. What could have been more appropriate!

In one's designing, not only is the idea important, but the things used to express the idea are vital to convey the mood. Clever use of materials won't help a weak design. Conversely, a good design concept is sabotaged if the materials used to carry it out are not perceptively chosen.

Unusual mixes of materials, if tastefully and adroitly used, astonish the onlooker and provide startling and pleasing surprises. You might use velvet with denim, burlap with lace, silks with cottons, rope with silky threads, wire with roving—the list could go on and on. A piece I did recently combined stuffed and quilted cotton ribbing with appliquéd areas of crushed velvets and stitchery done in gilt thread and pearl cotton. Although the mixture sounds quite odd, it works.

Don't hesitate to be daring in your approaches to carrying out design concepts. The worst that can happen is that the result does not please. In that case you will have learned what *not* to do in the future. Have a good time accumulating a challenging, stimulating, and esthetically pleasurable group of things with which to pursue your art. Handling, arranging, and rearranging—"doodling" with your materials will accelerate a flow of ideas, sometimes so many it's difficult to decide on any one specific problem or project. Then you will come to the realization that life is indeed too short!

3 Methods

Many methods of textile construction are employed when one begins experimentation in fiber art. People who are interested in stitchery and related procedures of fiber manipulation are usually familiar with the basic techniques to draw upon when expressing design ideas in the medium of fiber. Embroidery stitches, traditional simple crochet, functional knitting used in making wearing apparel, elementary patchwork, braiding (the kind used in making little girls' pigtails), smocking, gathering—most of these techniques, ancient in origin, are old friends to fiber-oriented folk. However, to ensure familiarity with the methods discussed in this book, some of them are briefly reviewed.

For the textile methods requiring sewing, a short explanation of needle differences may be helpful. In stitchery, especially when using the heavier yarns, it is necessary to use a needle with a large eye to accommodate the yarn. If the material chosen for a working surface is loosely woven (burlap, monk's cloth, homespun, etc.), blunt-pointed tapesty or yarn needles may work very well.

Needles are categorized into four types: sharp (small eye, used with sewing threads); crewel or embroidery (long eye, used with embroidery floss or perle—also known as "pearl"—cotton); chenille (large eye, used with thick threads and tapestry yarns); tapestry (long eye, blunt-pointed, used with any yarn which can be accepted by the eye). In all four groups, the smaller the needle number, the larger the needle.

In addition to this group of four needle types, there are many other kinds designed for specific purposes which may also be handy in stitchery. It is wise to have a large variety of needles in one's workbox so the appropriate tool is available to use when necessity demands. A few of the specialized needles are: sail-maker's; carpet; leather; upholsterer's, some of which are curved; yarn, made in both plastic and metal; quilting, which are very short with a tiny eye—so small my eyesight is not keen enough to use them; and even surgical suture needles. Try using these more unusual needles. You might discover the perfect tool to suit your way of working.

QUILTING

Quilting, the type of construction used in making the beautiful quilts which are currently enjoying a renaissance of popularity, is an extremely valuable textile procedure to use in experimental stitchery and in soft sculpture. Giving surface interest to wall hangings and soft sculpture, it emphasizes areas which one wishes to dramatize, resulting in highlights and shadows in fabric, especially noticeable in materials with a sheen. When one does a stitchery, then quilts sections of it, the whole character of the stitchery changes; it gains a depth and richness which the flat surface, prior to quilting, did not have.

The process of quilting is very easy. Three layers of material are super-imposed on one another. The top layer is the surface which can be plain, or on which you may have done stitchery motifs; the second layer can be one of many different kinds of cloth or fiber, depending on how thick you wish the quilting to be. Cotton, dacron, or polyester fiber filling (sometimes called batts) is readily available at fabric stores, needlework shops, and some ten-cent stores. It comes in rolls which can be cut in pieces of the desired size, and is very good for the filing or middle layer in quilting. You can also use worn-out turkish towels, flannel, old pieces of blanket, remnants of wool suiting, cut-out sections of discarded heavy clothing, and the like. If you want a very thin quilted effect you can simply use another piece of the same material you used for the top surface. The third layer in your "sandwich" is anything you wish to use to hold the filling (middle layer) in place. If it is visible and an integral part of your design you would want to choose a fabric complementary to the working surface (top layer). If not, then any material which will serve the purpose can be used.

Now your sandwich is complete (see Fig. 3.4). You are ready for the actual quilting, which is the process of sewing all three layers together. How you decide to do this depends on your design. If you have a stitchery or appliqué center of interest, you might wish to sew the layers together all around that focal point (see Fig. 3.5), emphasizing it by raising the surface. The thicker the middle layer is, the puffier the quilted section will be and the more visually prominent.

Fig. 3.1 *Snail*—quilted, stuffed, and stitched (Betsy Cannon).

Fig. 3.2 *Self-portrait*— quilted, stuffed, and appliquéd element (Betsy Cannon).

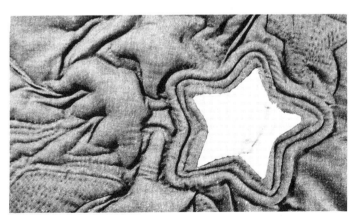

Fig. 3.3 Detail of *Self-portrait*.

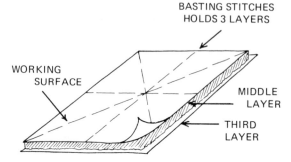

BASTING STITCHES
HOLDS 3 LAYERS

WORKING
SURFACE

MIDDLE
LAYER

THIRD
LAYER

Fig. 3.4 Quilting layers.

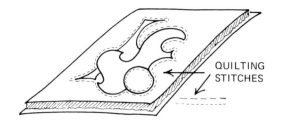

QUILTING
STITCHES

Fig. 3.5 Quilting stitches.

The stitch used in your quilting is a matter of choice, dependent upon the design concept. If you want the area being puffed to rely on the surface stitchery and (or) applique for interest, you would probably decide upon a running stitch, using small stitches in thread matching the working surface that would blend in and be practically invisible. On the other hand, if you wish the quilting itself to be part of the design or the entire design, without stitchery or appliqué, try using contrasting colors with a large running stitch or an embroidery stitch, such as a feather stitch or chain stitch, squared chain, cretan, or any other simple embroidery stitch which seems appropriate. It is advisable to use heavy-duty thread to avoid the nuisance of breaking threads when doing the quilting, and to run the thread over a piece of beeswax for additional strength before using it.

STUFFING

Spot-stuffing areas on a work is a variation of quilting. Instead of spreading the filling over the entire wrong side of the working surface, select the individual areas which you want to accentuate and put the second layer in those areas only. A very handy material to use for this purpose is ''loose'' polyester fiber filling which comes in bags, ready to take out handfuls as needed. Most ten-cent stores seem to carry this material and it is not expensive.

When a decision is made concerning the sections of your work you wish to stuff, and the filling is positioned, cut a small piece of any thin cloth and cover the filling, sewing it in place. After the hanging is finished you will

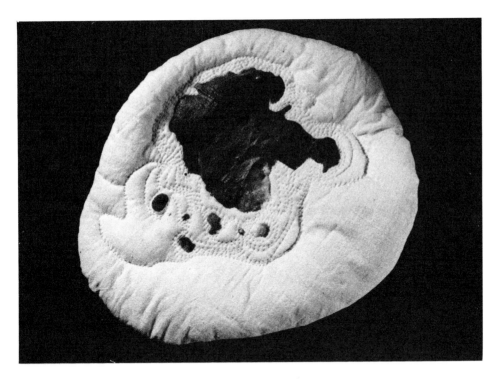

Fig. 3.6 Wall-piece with melted crayon motif, stuffed and quilted (Betsy Cannon).

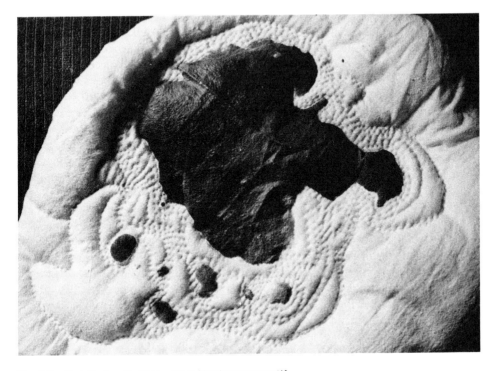

Fig. 3.7 Detail of wall-piece with melted crayon motif.

probably want to line (cover) the entire wrong side, thus hiding the small stuffed portions. If so, the material covering the filling can be basted to hold it temporarily (see Fig. 3.8) and the basting thread removed once the piece is worked and ready to be lined. Make certain that a few inconspicuous stitches are taken to hold the small covering pieces of cloth in place so they do not shift when the basting stitches are removed. If you don't want to line the work, these small third-layer pieces of cloth can be sewn to the working surface with small stitches and matching thread. The stitches will blend inconspicuously into the color of the working surface and be almost unnoticeable. But in the interests of good craftsmanship, which includes a proper finish for one's works, lining is recommended, especially when you have included small stuffed elements.

APPLIQUÉ

Appliqué, found in many old-fashioned sewing and needlework books that feature directions for making functional household items and trimming for clothing, is an excellent technique when interpreted in a contemporary way. It involves sewing one or more pieces of cloth onto a working surface. The cloth shapes one uses can be representational or abstract and can overlap one another in any way desirable to develop a good design concept.

When you start to design an appliquéd hanging, you may wish to make a few sketches as preliminary planning or you may prefer to work entirely spontaneously, letting the design evolve as you arrange and rearrange the shapes. Once the arrangement of the shapes is adjusted to your satisfaction, pin or baste them in place so they are not displaced while being sewed down.

There are several ways in which to sew down appliquéd pieces. One of the most common is to turn under the edges of your pieces ⅛-¼ inch, baste the edges down, and using a small running stitch just inside the turned-in edge, top-sew the piece to your working foundation (see Fig. 3.9). If the edges of the applique piece are curved, it will be necessary to cut little slashes 1/16 inch or so at right angles to the edge along the curved section so you can turn that edge under with no bunching (see Fig. 3.10). A whipped diagonal stitch is also a good way of attaching a shape to a surface (see Fig. 3.11). If you would like to get a free, less structural look in your appliquéd design, you might try sewing the pieces on the backing with raw edges showing, eliminating turning the edges under. This method is especially nice if your shapes are of material which frays interestingly. You can use the frayed edge as a design component. The stitch you use to sew the shape down can be a running stitch or one of the embroidery stitches. You can also use clusters of French knots to attach the appliqué. You need not stitch around the entire edge; some edges can be left free as long as the piece is held securely (see Fig. 3.12). This last approach, however, would not be a practical method for use in clothing or anything else that goes in and out of a washer, or is intended for hard usage. One has to use

Methods

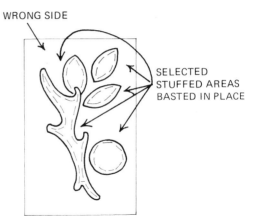

WRONG SIDE

SELECTED
STUFFED AREAS
BASTED IN PLACE

Fig. 3.8   Basting stuffed areas.

RUNNING STITCH JUST
INSIDE TURNED UNDER
EDGES

Fig. 3.9   Sewing down appliquéd areas.

SLASHED CURVED
EDGES TO GET
SMOOTH TURNED
UNDER EDGES

Fig. 3.10   Turning under curved edges.

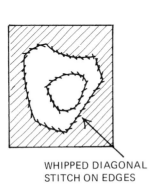

WHIPPED DIAGONAL
STITCH ON EDGES

Fig. 3.11   Whipped diagonal
stitch on edges.

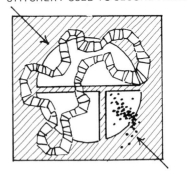

STITCHERY USED TO SECURE PIECES

FRENCH KNOTS SECURING PIECE

Fig. 3.12   Securing appliqué with
stitchery and French knots.

good judgment in the sewing method chosen in terms of compatibility with function and care.

You may prefer to do the actual sewing of your appliqué "in hand," that is, working while holding it in your hands, using the fingers to spread flat the spot where sewing is being done. Or, if a taut surface is desired—and this is preferable, especially when working on a large design—a hoop or canvas stretchers (the latter available in art supply stores, some stationers, and fabric shops) can be used. With canvas stretchers the material is thumbtacked to the frame before working on it. Recently, I finished seventy-two quilt blocks, each featuring a different appliquéd abstract design. They measure about 10″ X 12″ and in stitching on pieces this small I found working in hand completely satisfactory. The material could be spread flat by the fingers of the holding hand so there was no puckering of the appliqué and stitchery. In larger hangings I use canvas stretchers.

REVERSE APPLIQUÉ

Reverse appliqué is a variation of the conventional appliqué method with which many of us are familiar. Lovely and intricate examples of reverse appliqué are the molas, the work of the Cuna Indians in Panama and Colombia. These designs, used in the colorful clothing worn by the Cuna Indians, have prompted many admiring tourists to bring samples of their work back to the United States as mementos of their visits in those regions. The technique used in reverse appliqué generated the interest of fiber artists who adapted the method to their own contemporary designing.

The process, used by the Cuna Indians, is rather complex and requires some advance planning unlike some of the other types of textile construction. Put on top of one another two or more layers of closely woven cloth—cotton percale is a good choice—in different colors. The sharper the color contrasts of the layers the more vibrant the design will be, almost to the point of gaudiness. To get a subtler, more sophisticated result, you may wish to choose a color scheme close in color range and more subdued in tone. A layering of shades of one color, a monochromatic color scheme, works up well. When the layers are in place, baste them all together so there is no shifting. Then cut away the first shape (see Fig. 3.13) revealing the second layer in the series. Turn the edges under and sew them inconspicuously with a hemming stitch in matching color thread. Then cut into the second layer, always turning the edges under and sewing in place as you proceed (see Fig. 3.14), and so on. You can see that this method is quite structured and not amenable to changes once the cuts have been made, hence the need for an advance planned design in mind or worked out on paper. Save all your cut-out pieces as they may be used for surface appliqué as the design develops. Stitchery, of course, can also be used, and if you wish additional interest, some of the top appliquéd pieces can be lightly stuffed to give surface relief providing a rather nice counterpoint to the cut-away areas.

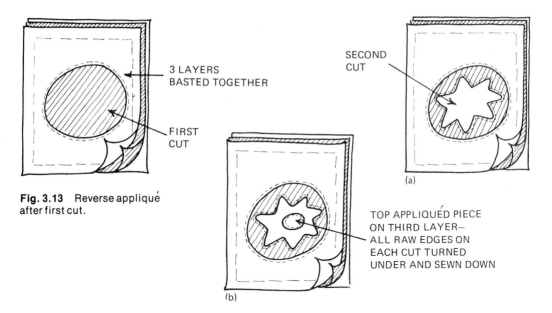

Fig. 3.13 Reverse appliqué after first cut.

3 LAYERS BASTED TOGETHER

FIRST CUT

SECOND CUT

(a)

TOP APPLIQUÉD PIECE ON THIRD LAYER—ALL RAW EDGES ON EACH CUT TURNED UNDER AND SEWN DOWN

(b)

Fig. 3.14 Reverse appliqué after second cut.

Another idea to consider when doing reverse appliqué is to use as one of your layers a printed fabric to vary the traditional use of only plain colors.

PATCHWORK

Closely allied with appliqué is patchwork which has been revived for contemporary use in the design of clothing, wall hangings, pillows, as well as in modern quilts and even sleeping bags.

The patchwork technique is very simple. It involves the sewing together of separate pieces of cloth to make a larger piece. In the case of a quilt the "larger" piece is *very* large, indeed!

Pin or baste together a group of patches of varying but compatible prints and (or) solids. Check the resulting overall color effect to see if you want to reposition any pieces before sewing them together. The sewing may be done either by machine or by hand. The effect achieved by hand sewing, because of the slight variations in stitching, is different and, to my taste, more desirable than that resulting from machine sewing—the same difference one discerns between a hand-thrown pot and one made by machine. Seam together all the pieces, using a simple fine running stitch. When all the sewing is finished, press open the seams carefully and iron out your large piece of patchwork.

The shapes of the pieces patched together is, of course, at the discretion of the designer. These shapes can be simple geometric forms with a disciplined, structured result, or "crazy quilt" pieces, like those used in Victorian quilts,

33

which differed greatly in shape, with no effort made to achieve any particular overall design. The crazy quilt was a good way to use up a lot of irregularly shaped scraps of cloth and the end results were surprisingly attractive considering the unplanned nature of the project. The Victorian quilts usually featured a lot of stitchery on top of the patchwork. Joinings of the patches were often covered with an embroidery stitch, such as feather, cretan, buttonhole, or blanket, with additional stitching on the patches themselves.

HOOKING

When working out design ideas for stitcheries, variety of texture is an important quality to consider. One way to get interesting texture and one which is easily intermingled with other techniques is hooking, the same procedure used in making rugs. It is necessary to choose a loosely woven fabric or rug canvas for the hooked portion of your design so the hooking needle can be easily drawn in and out.

If the main portion of your design is being worked on a tightly woven material, you can do a hooked portion as a separate element, joining it to the rest of the piece when it is finished. I have done this on several occasions, using rug canvas for the hooked section and sewing it to the primary piece afterward with no difficulty. You can, of course, sew loosely woven fabric, destined to be hooked to the rest of the hanging prior to its being hooked. Either way is practical.

There are several types of needles which can be used in hooking: the hand hook, the punch needle, speed hooks such as the eggbeater and the shuttle hook, and an electric needle (expensive). For stitchery, one need not invest in an expensive or complicated tool. I have found that a hand hook or a punch needle are easy to use, efficient, and obtain the desired effect at minimum cost. Complete directions for use are supplied with punch needles as well as with speed needles. With a hand hook, holding it at any angle comfortable to you, pull up loops of yarn from the wrong side of the canvas or cloth to the working surface which is right side up. From the wrong side, the yarn is held with the left hand (reverse if you are left-handed) and fed to the needle which is then drawn up through the fabric. Unlike the punch needle, you may use short lengths of yarn. After you hook the part of the design intended for this texture the loops may be cut so they hang down in strands, left as loops, or you may use a mixture of each technique. Cutting the loops tends to intensify yarn color, making it look brighter. You may wish to pull your loops through unevenly to get greater variety in length of the pile. The long cut strands can be yarn-wrapped which is a nice finish, or left as they are (see Fig. 3.15).

When using a punch needle, thread it with a length of yarn 1½-2 yards long. When you hold the needle perpendicular to the canvas or cloth with the wrong side upright, the slotted side of the needle faces the direction in which you are working as you push it through the fabric as far as it will go, forming a loop on the under side. Hold the loops with thumb and index finger on the under side (which is the right side) as you work so they aren't pulled back out

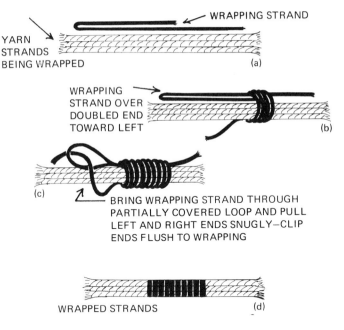

WRAPPING STRAND

YARN
STRANDS
BEING WRAPPED

(a)

WRAPPING
STRAND OVER
DOUBLED END
TOWARD LEFT

(b)

(c)

BRING WRAPPING STRAND THROUGH
PARTIALLY COVERED LOOP AND PULL
LEFT AND RIGHT ENDS SNUGLY—CLIP
ENDS FLUSH TO WRAPPING

WRAPPED STRANDS

(d)

Fig. 3.15 Yarn-wrapped strands.

again as the needle is pulled up, ready for the next thrust. Here again, once the loops are made and you have finished hooking the section, they can be cut and (or) left uncut.

When hooking it is important that the working surface of the backing be taut. If you plan a large hooked hanging, some kind of a frame will be necessary on which to tack down the fabric. You can use canvas stretchers, mentioned in the section on appliqué, thumbtacking the edges of the fabric used for hooking to the stretchers. You can also make a simple frame of wood pieces and lace the work to the frame if it is too small to thumbtack (see Fig. 3.16). Hooking tends to distort the material being worked so it is pulled out of shape. Firmly tacking or lacing it in place while in work will correct that situation.

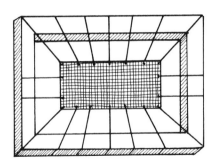

Fig. 3.16 Small piece of canvas/
cloth laced to wood frame. Use
thumbtacks or small nails on back
of frame for tying lacing strings.

When choosing the yarns with which to hook consider the possibilties of using twines, ribbons, raffia, leather or plastic strips, or anything else which can be pulled through the backing to get unusual effects.

SIMPLE CROCHET

For the purposes of experimental fiber work, crochet is an invaluable technique to develop form, texture, and high relief as well as a way to get open, free-form spatial relationships in threads. Unlike the crochet used in functional work, with the emphasis sometimes placed on virtuosity of pattern, in stitchery work one need known only the simplest crochet stitches to have this tool at one's command.

Chaining, single and double crochet with their variations are the basis for use in the kind of fiber experimentation with which this book deals. You will find, after being comfortable doing these stitches, you can even improvise your own variations should you be inspired to do so. For in-depth knowledge of crochet and a wide vocabulary of stitches consult the Bibliography where several excellent sources are recommended.

When learning to crochet choose a rather large hook to work with, perhaps a #7 or a #10. Sizes of hooks vary from very small (lower numbers) to accommodate the fine threads used in delicate lace-making, to quite large, suitable for heavy twines and small robes. Hooks are available from ten-cent stores, yarn and needlework shops, and variety stores and can be obtained in wood, plastic, or metal. Some hooks are sized by letter, A-K, small to large, "H" is a good learning size. Wood tools are esthetically pleasing, but I've broken the hook end of a couple of my favorite #10s when crocheting vigorously with jute, so I wouldn't recommend them for heavy work. Metal is most durable; plastic sometimes bends and breaks. Metal would seem to be the most practical choice.

With the large hook use a sturdy yarn, wool worsted, rug yarn, or heavy string. Working with a large hook and heavy yarn (or its equivalent) is easier when learning; you can readily see how the yarn is forming into the loops without straining. After you are familiar with the process you can then try working with the finer yarns and threads. Recently I spent several weeks trying out different effects resulting from using double-thickness sewing thread and a large hook, adjusting the tension from very loose to very tight—even switching occasionally to a small hook for some of the areas—to get open spider-weblike filaments combined with tight filled-in sections. The look was so intriguing I made several wall hangings using this approach. There are many interesting effects one can get by combining unlikely hook and yarn sizes once the crocheting process is mastered.

Hold your hook as you would a pencil between thumb and index finger, the yarn held in the other hand, with the yarn over the top of the index finger which controls the tension, and then down between your thumb and

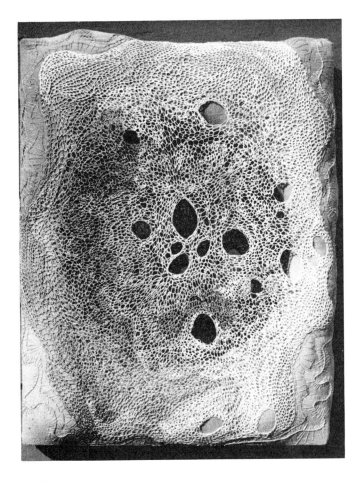

Fig. 3.17 *Yellow Tracery*—crocheted sewing thread in shades of yellow, with stitchery accents (author).

Fig. 3.18 Detail of *Yellow Tracery*.

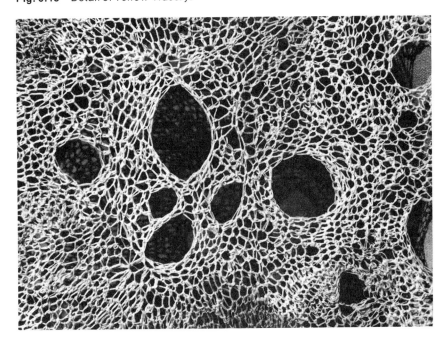

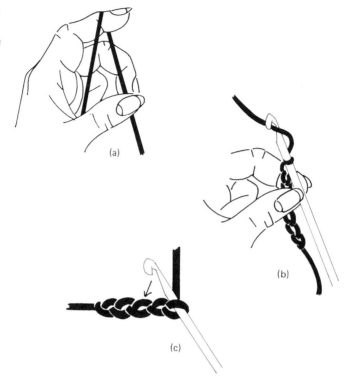

Fig. 3.19 (a) Crochet technique: thread tension controlled by holding yarn as illustrated: over index finger, down and held by middle finger and thumb; (b) chaining by drawing yarn with crochet hook through loop on hook—hold chaining as shown; (c) beginning single crochet—insert hook second loop from right (see arrow). Abbreviations in crochet: CH—Chain; SC—Single crochet; DC—double crochet; HDC—Half double crochet.

middle finger where it is held (see Fig. 3.19). Insert the hook into the thread on your index finger (toward the fingernail) and twist it back facing you. Your thread will be crossed. Draw the thread from the ball end—not the short end—through the loop formed by the twist and pull on the short end held by thumb and index finger. You now have a knotted loop from which to begin to chain. With your hook, draw another loop from the thread which is on the far side of your index finger and so on. You are now chaining which is the foundation stitch upon which to build succeeding rows of crochet [see Fig. 3.19(b)]. When crocheting with very heavy yarns, twines, twisted cords, and similar materials you can grasp your hook in your fist as you would grasp a good-sized screwdriver. This prevents strain on the index finger when working with tough, firm yarns. I've found the "screwdriver grip" preferable when working with jute, sisal, and other like twines. For finer work the traditional hook hold is satisfactory.

When you have a line of chained stitches you are ready to do single

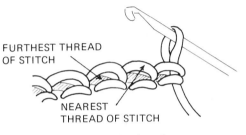

FURTHEST THREAD
OF STITCH

NEAREST
THREAD OF STITCH

Fig. 3.20 Choosing ridge locations.

crochet. The foundation line of chaining should be at least six inches long so it is easy to hang on to. Holding the line of chaining between our thumb and middle finger as shown in Figure 3.19(b), insert your hook in the loop second from the end [see Fig. 3.19(c)], yarn under the hook and draw through. You now have two loops on the hook. Again, lay the yarn under the hook and draw through the two loops on the hook; this will result in one loop being left on the hook. Repeat the process with the next chain loop and so on, until you come to the end of your foundation of chained loops. Try to work loosely so you can see what is happening to the yarn as it is being worked. When you reach the end of the line lay the yarn once again over the hook and draw it through to make an extra chained loop to facilitate turning to begin the next (second) row. This extra loop at the end keeps the edges even. If you did not do this your piece of crochet would gradually decrease in width which is one way of shaping. To being the second row turn your work around and repeat the first row. If you wish to get a horizontal ridged effect when continuing on with the rows, instead of inserting your hook in the openings with the *two* threads of the preceding stitch on top of your hook, you insert it under only *one*. If it is the one nearest you, the ridge will appear on the under side. If you insert in the further one, the ridge will appear on the side facing you at the moment (see Fig. 3.20). Practice chaining and single crochet until you feel at ease with them. Soon the process will become almost automatic and you can divert your attention from what your hands are doing toward what you are trying to say with the product of your hands.

For half-double crochet, which is a way of slightly lengthening the stitch, you lay the yarn from the back of the hook under the hook, and then insert it into the opening. (The opening into which the hook is inserted is very obvious, especially when working with heavy yarn.) Drawn the yarn through; this will give you three loops on the hook. Again draw the yarn through (as with single crochet) the *three* loops. This gives you a higher stitch. For double crochet, repeat the procedure for the half-double stitch with the following difference: instead of drawing the yarn through the three loops on the hook all at once, draw the yarn through *two*; you now have two loops on the hook. Lay the yarn under your hook as when beginning the half-double, and draw through the two loops, leaving one loop on the hook. This gives an even higher stitch. An excellent little book to refer to when learning to crochet is an inexpensive paperback called *A Complete Guide to Crochet Stitches*, by Mary M. Dawson. With these simple stitches, the possibilities for development of design ideas in fiber are considerably broadened. To prevent a piece of crochet from raveling when finished, cut the yarn a few inches away from the last loop worked, lay the cut end under the hook, draw through that end loop and tighten into a knot.

SIMPLE BRAIDING AND KNOTTING

The use of braids is a useful and interesting way of manipulating fibrous, plastic, leather, or any flexible strands. Recently I saw a handsome floor sculpture made of combined braids and long, free-falling strands of hand-dyed yarns. Called *Reflections on the American Southwest,* executed by Brooke Stevens, it was shown in the "Fiberworks" exhibition at Boston City Hall in 1975. Although very simple in technique, it was an extremely effective self-supporting column of beautiful muted colors streaming down from a height of about twelve feet. One need not be so entranced with complex textile construction that the simpler methods are neglected. Sometimes their simplicity is more effective in the long run.

To do a simple three-strand braid (see Fig. 3.22, strands designated A, B, and C) you lay the right-hand strand C, over the middle strand, B, crossing them. Then lay the left-hand strand, A, over the right-hand strand, C, crossing them. The middle strand, B (which is now at the far right), is brought over the left strand (which was crossed over the right strand) and cross. The right strand, C, is crossed over the middle, B, and so on. If you try this with heavy yarn or twine you can readily see what is going on with the braid. This sort of braiding, the "hair-braid" type, is very effective when used with cords of two or more colors, or when done with groups of cords, each group serving as separate units with which to work. In a piece where braids are a component of the design, you might consider changing the scale of the braids while working to get more variety in the piece. Make a series of contiguous small braids. Then using the individual braided strands for working units, braid the braids into a large, more dramatic presentation of that component.

Another thing you can do with braids is to make a series of small ones, then knot them in a square knot, a Josephine knot, or other more intricate kinds of knots. To make a square knot using three strands place the right-hand cord, bringing it under the center cord, and diagonally up, under, and through the space (on the right side) between the middle cord and the right-hand cord (see Fig. 3.23). You have now completed the first half of the square knot, which is called the half-knot or half-square knot. If you repeated this step over and over you would get a very attractive spiral twist. The full square knot is flat. To complete the square knot you go on to the second half of the procedure as follows: place the right-hand cord under the central cord, horizontally. Place the left-hand cord, under the right-hand cord, bringing it up diagonally over the center cord, and through (from the

Fig. 3.21 *As Happy as Kings*—stuffed, stitched wall-piece with braids (Mary Tibbals Ventre; photograph by Mowbray-Clarke & Campbell, courtesy of Little, Brown and Company).

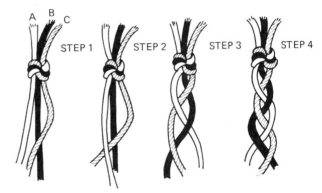

Fig. 3.22 Braiding.

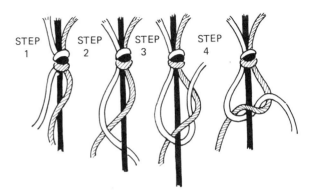

Fig. 3.23 Braids with square knots.

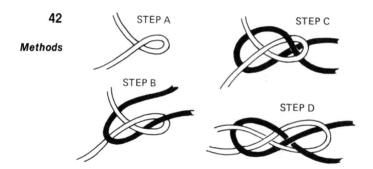

Fig. 3.24 Josephine knot.

top) the space between the center and right-hand cords. Draw the knot together. You will have an attractive flat knot, the kind used in macramé.

To do a Josephine knot, sometimes referred to as a Carrick Bend, you proceed as follows: using two cords, make a loop with the left cord [see Fig. 3.24 (Step A)]. Bring the right cord behind the loop and over the end of left cord, below the loop [Fig. 3.24 (Step B)]. Bring the right cord above and behind the loop. (It's a bit tricky from now on so note the diagram carefully.) Continue downward on a diagonal, over the next cord encountered [Fig. 3.24 (Step D)] and, still heading down on a diagonal, under the next cord and over the last. Pull slightly to align the knot. It is an interwoven knot which may be left quite loose or pulled snugly in place as desired. This knot is lovely when done with a silky cord, such as rattail or parachute cord.

GATHERING

The charming old-fashioned little girls' dresses trimmed with smocking are an inspiration for a free, textural quality in fiber achieved by gathering fabric into puckers. While the smocking used on clothing is very precise and structured, its contemporary cousin is spontaneous in look (even though sometimes deliberately planned as a design component) and is very relevant to today's fiber statements. A handsome hanging seen in Boston City Hall in 1975 was a piece done by Shirley Fink, a teacher in the Artisans Program at Boston University and an outstanding weaver in the New England area. The piece involved considerable gathering up or pulling of a neutral-hued fabric. Although other design components were used, the puckering of the fabric was the dominant element in my view.

The process of gathering is very easy. A running stitch is placed where you wish to pucker the cloth, and then pulled as tightly as is desired. You can plan a series of gathers following a preconceived design or gather at random, then design around the result using it as a nucleus for further amplification.

Fig. 3.25 Ridging.

RIDGING

Ridging is another method of achieving texture in fiber and involves random seaming at right angles to the working surface. If it is done on materials with a sheen or that change in depth of color as they are folded, twisted, or crumpled (such as velvet, satin, brocade, taffeta, silk, or corduroy), the effect will be much more dramatic than with matte finish fabrics.

To ridge, you pinch together a fold in the cloth, treating it as you would a seam. The width of the fold can be as variable as the design demands. Pin the fold, directing it where you wish it to go, then sew along the seam as you would if you were seaming together any two pieces of cloth (see Fig. 3.25). You will note the interplay of light and shadow and the enriched quality of the working surface in the ridged areas.

PULLING

In loosely woven materials such as burlap, monk's cloth, and similar fabrics, a pleasing texture can be obtained by pulling threads here and there in the cloth; this will cause it to pucker up in much the same way as when gathering with a running stitch, and is much faster. You are, however, limited in direction as the threads go only vertically and horizontally. In gathering by running stitch you can go in any direction you wish.

If any of the preceding techniques intrigue you to the point of wanting to learn more about them, it is suggested that you consult the Bibliography at the back of this book. There are excellent books dealing fully with specific techniques and providing detailed instructions for advanced learning in case you aspire to be a virtuoso in any one particular fiber method.

When working with fiber, it is very easy to equate excellence of workmanship with good design. Each is essential to create fine art statements, whatever the medium. It is also easy to fall into the trap of overdoing and overworking an idea—to elaborate on the idea until the whole concept is blurred and lost among a welter of techniques. Avoid putting everything you know in one piece! Some of the most moving, most beautiful, and most eloquent fiber statements are those which are simply but superbly worked. One should strive for excellent craftsmanship in execution and to be a good technician, able to render an idea well. After you have mastered your technique, remember that taste, judgment, and sound knowledge of design

44

principles are essential to transform the technician into the artist, to enable you to create, from a pile of materials, a new substantive, valid entity. Decoration will never make a poor design a good one; decoration *can*, however, weaken and even destroy a basically good design. When in doubt about whether or not to add a new element to a work, delay doing it. Let it rest for a few days; then look at it with a fresh eye to determine whether or not the piece really needs that element. Don't confuse the issue!

4 How to Begin

When first beginning experimentation with stitchery and the many textile construction methods, the mind is often in a turmoil of a design ideas. One idea leads to another and yet another until it seems as if a whole lifetime is too short to allow for exploration of them all. It is exciting to realize the range of possibilities when using conventional methods in these new, contemporary, inventive ways. Often it is difficult to settle down and focus your attention to one particular idea. For this reason, I find it desirable to keep several different projects going at the same time, each one in a different technique or combinations thereof. I can work, as the spirit moves, on whatever piece is most interesting to me at the moment. Ideas keep flowing when working in this way, with the inspiration gained while working on one specific piece spinning off toward the others in progress.

When experiencing a flow of ideas it is wise to jot them down. The design notebook mentioned in Chapter 1 is an ideal place to record inspirations before they are forgotten. Consider these jottings as a design bank from which to draw should you encounter a "dry spell" with a paucity of ideas.

There are other ways of kindling the imagination when the mental well runs dry. One which I frequently try when in this situation is to assemble a group of related materials—fabrics, several kinds of interesting yarns and threads, all in a harmonious color scheme. Arranging, rearranging, and handling visually and tactilely pleasing things usually results in some point of departure from which to begin a stitchery. As you move these materials about, keep in mind good design principles: dominance, balance, rhythm, proportion, unity, and contrast. After arriving at a satisfactory composition pin it in place, then tack it down with a few inconspicuous sewing stitches to hold it. Using this arrangement as a design nucleus, and working from the core of the design outward, begin the stitchery. Don't work from the outer edges of the working surface inward toward the design core. If you do, it is very easy to lose the focus of the design and, instead, to be confronted with a motley collection of disparate elements that are difficult to unify. Strive for design coherence as you work along, pausing before adding new areas of stitching to check for unity. Because this is a spontaneous way of working, the design will evolve as you progress, which is very exciting. You are continually confronted with a growing, changing entity, demanding new decisions as it develops.

Going back to the design notebook for a moment: if the book has been filled with a variety of materials—clippings, pictures, drawings, color and design notes, perhaps pressed plant parts, poetry, quotations, philosophical ruminations, swatches of cloth, and paper—it is a valuable aid for generating design ideas. It is also helpful to browse through books and periodicals on the various aspects of fiber art as well as those dealing generally with art and design. In addition, I've found books on architecture, sculpture, and photography to be excellent sources of ideas. All these stimuli will keep the mind fertile and susceptible to the creative process.

Another useful device for getting a stitchery design under way is to choose a piece of yarn about 12 inches long, and drop it on the cloth you intend to use as a working surface. Thick-and-thin or nubbly yarns are especially good for this; they are so interesting in themselves. After dropping the yarn on the cloth study the resulting linear shapes, the enclosed spaces, and the areas surrounding those enclosures. If the composition pleases you as it is, pin it down before it becomes disarranged, then couch it down with sewing thread and small sewing stitches if you don't want the couching itself to be a part of the design. When the design you get when you first drop the yarn needs repositioning, move the yarn around on the cloth until you like the overall shapes; fasten it down. The abstract appearance of the designs resulting from casual yarn drops are fun to work up and amplify with stitchery. Again, remember to work from the central part of the design outward. Fill in some of the enclosed spaces where you want a solid shape, choosing the stitch appropriate to the desired effect. When the yarn outline is worked up with the positive (filled-in) spaces and negative spaces (those left open and unworked) in good balance, work on the area outside the yarn outline. As you do the stitchery along the edges outside the outline, deviate from the outline if you care to, then reconverge with it at another point in the design, thus creating new spaces to be filled with stitchery or left open as your judgment dictates. Here again, as you work freely on a constantly evolving design with all the problems each additional change entails, you

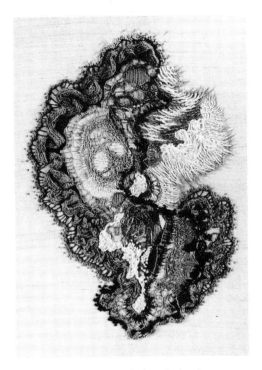

Fig. 4.1 *Terrain*—wandering abstract stitchery with knitted tubing (author).

will find the challenge exciting and stimulating. Sometimes it is hard to put the work aside to attend to the mundane chores and interruptions of everyday living. One can really get lost in one's work (which makes the fiber arts good therapy for people with problems). The joy of working with the hands, combined with the mental effort involved in creating one's own designs, can provide surcease from the sometimes overwhelming life situations which threaten us all at one time or another.

An effective method of building a design is to manipulate a fabric by twisting, crumpling, folding, pleating, gathering, ridging or in any manner "distressing" the cloth you can devise. Sew the distorted cloth to the material planned for use as a foundation working surface and use this interesting texture as a catalyst from which to plan the rest of the design. The options for augmenting this kind of textured surface are many. Stuffing, adding crocheted elements, stitchery, and needle-weaving are all possibilities. You can probably come up with more. (Instructions for needle-weaving are discussed further on in Chapter 10.)

One idea that I've used is to make separate modules and attach them to the design as a focal point, adding stitchery as the design demands (see Fig. 4.3). Modules are very easy to make. Cut a piece of cloth in a roughly circular shape and run a gathering thread around the edge; pull slightly to

Fig. 4.2 Design class exercise with crumpled fabric and wrapped yarn fall (Martha Liller).

Fig. 4.3 *The Shattered Heart*—stuffed modules, crumpled fabric, crochet (author).

get a cuplike shape; fill the cup with polyester fiber filling, draw the gathering thread up snugly, and fasten. Determine ahead of time the approximate size you want the module to be and cut the circular shape large enough to get that size when it is gathered and filled. If you want the modules to be exactly round with no irregularities in shape, use a circular template to use as a gauge when cutting the cloth. Sometimes, however, the less than perfect circles make more interesting modules.

When stuffing a crumpled texture, analyze it, deciding where you want the emphasis to be. On the wrong side of the work, push out that section and put polyester filling in the cavity(ies). Cover with a small piece of cloth (see Chapter 3, the section on spot stuffing) and sew in place, keeping the filling from being dislodged. Now check the right side of the work to see if you got the effect you wanted. Stitchery can then be added for accentuation as well as to provide an additional element.

Crocheting along or on top of the folds or ridges of distressed fabric is another way to gain visual impact. It will be necessary to put in a line of stitches to serve as a foundation line in which to insert the crochet hook **48** wherever you want to crochet. A chain stitch is a good one to use for this purpose. When the line of stitches has been established you are ready to crochet. Thread a needle with the yarn you plan to use for the crocheting and draw the short end of the yarn from the right side of the work through to the wrong side and knot the end. Remove the needle; the yarn is now fastened to the wrong side and is in place on the right side for crocheting. Insert the crochet hook under the first chain stitch and draw a loop of yarn through. Lay the yarn under the hook and again in the next chain stitch and draw the yarn through the two loops on the hook (see Chapter 3, the section on crocheting). The chain stitching is only used as a foundation for the first row. When you reach the end of the line of chain stitches, add an extra crochet loop. Turn and crochet back in that first row to form the second row and so on until the crocheted element is of a satisfactory height in relation to the work as a whole. If crocheting directly on the working surface seems too awkward, try making a separate crocheted piece and then sewing it to the main design. I've had good results doing it both ways.

Problem-solving stretches the imagination and challenges the artist's ingenuity to provide solutions. When casting around for inspiration it is a good learning experience to deliberately set oneself some kind of limited design problem; then try to solve it with originality, inventiveness, and artistic validity.

A demanding stitchery problem is working out a design using one stitch only, relying on variations in that stitch for interest. Careful consideration of materials and colors chosen to accompany the stitchery will be very helpful in avoiding monotony in the finished result. Strive for the unusual rather than the obvious solution to any problem you tackle; don't take the easy way out and stint on thoughtfulness and careful study of your problem. Overcoming difficulties can only be a positive factor in the growth of any artist. A member of my experimental stitchery workshop did a wall hanging using only French knots for her interpretation, relying for interest on textural buildup of the knots, thickly piled upon one another and on overall design shapes (see Figs. 4.4 and 4.5). The subdued color scheme used was also limited—soft beiges and browns with rusty orange accents. The visually successful piece is inviting tactilely, too, because of the rough knotted surface.

A rich stitchery stratum can be built up by layering randomly placed straight stitches on the foundation cloth. Relying on careful use of color, judicious placement of lights and darks, with varying yarn weights, crosshatch the straight stitches (see Fig. 4.6) thickly. Note how the colors are working with each other, adding lights and darks where needed. Stand a few feet away from the work every so often to gauge the general effect of the colorplay. This way you can see where the color emphasis is being placed as the work progresses, and add lighter or darker values where needed for good balance. The single-stitch exercise is fun to do; the appearance of the work is continually changing as more stitches are added and the final result is a surface of depth and richness. This particular problem has two parts: (1) building a shape by straight-stitch placement, and (2) working with color to achieve depth and harmony.

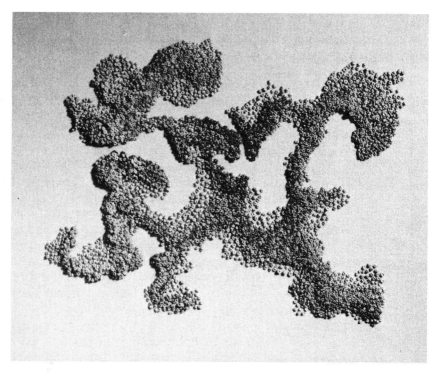

Fig. 4.4 *The Third Day*—stitchery using French knots only (Martha Liller).

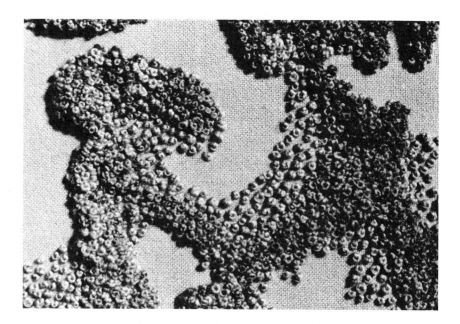

Fig. 4.5 Detail of *The Third Day*.

Fig. 4.6 Crosshatched stitching.

Fig. 4.7 Round untitled—limited to variations of spider web stitch and French knots (Martha Liller).

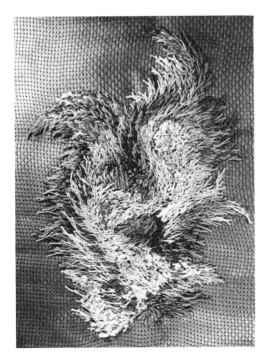

Fig. 4.8 Stitchery stratum of built-up straight stitches, French knots (author).

Another problem you might like to try is to work with a monochromatic color scheme—choosing a backing and yarns and threads of varying shades of one color only. In this situation, reliance on interesting stitch use, types of yarns, and perhaps other methods of fabric manipulation can forestall a monotonous presentation. Although you will need adroit stitching, using variations in the stitches chosen, try not to use too many different kinds of stitches in one piece. Otherwise a busy, incoherent result is almost assured. Use several types of yarn and threads ranging from thin to thick, perhaps including some of the nubbly yarns and those with slubs. You may decide to distress some cloth and attach it to the working (foundation) surface; consider using a crocheted element as an adjunct. There are many possible solutions to this problem. Analyze the design to determine which would best serve that design. The value of deliberate limitation in working out a fiber piece lies in the necessity for improvisation—the need to really think about what you are doing, to consider the possibilities, and to make choices.

Frequently, while working on a project, you reach a point in the work where you don't know what to do next. You are stuck. It is easy at these moments to yield to the temptation to add little details just because you feel you must do *something* although you are unsure of what that something should be. Adding little touches here and little elements there in a helter-skelter way, lacking assurance of their necessity to the design, is a very good way to ruin it. It is at this stage that many potentially good pieces are spoiled by trivia. Each design element included in the work should be carefully considered and thoughtfully added; no element should function merely as a vehicle to extricate oneself from the mire of indecision.

Having said all that, what is one to do when roadblocks occur? The most important thing, I feel, is to put the work aside for a few days. When working closely on a project one becomes so involved with it that judgment is clouded and objectivity is temporarily lost. A short time away from the work enables one to view it with refreshed eye, mind, and spirit. Sometimes the solution to the seemingly unsurmountable impasse becomes so clear that one wonders how it could have once seemed so perplexing.

Charging the creative batteries by all sorts of stimuli, whether they be books, periodicals, or visits to fiber exhibitions and art galleries, is, I've found personally, a good way to keep the creative juices flowing, to keep the level of excitement high. This is not to suggest that one should copy someone else's idea or turn out work that is derivative. However, it is important to keep abreast of the current developments in the fiber world and to be inspired by what others are doing in the field. Talking with other artists is gratifying. By so doing, one is reassured that the difficulties encountered in one's own work are shared by almost everyone else doing similar work. There is comfort in this. Then, too, in conversation with other fiber artists there is inevitably some "brainstorming," with input of ideas from one's colleagues. We can help each other; we can encourage each other; we can give moral support to each other—and we should.

A good way to increase personal artistic growth, especially when work has been put aside to gain a fresh perspective on it, is to use this time for experimentation with new techniques. There are so many "new" methods to explore (many of which are really old ways resurrected), one often feels there is never enough time to learn them all. So, when a block of time is at your disposal, use it to learn something new to add to your creative tool chest. Make several small pieces utilizing that unfamiliar technique; play with it until you feel you have stretched it to its limits. Be unconcerned with result and become thoroughly immersed in process. Time spent in experimentation, free from the constraints inherent in turning out a finished piece, is valuable. It is learning and growing time. Take advantage of all these periods when your work is not going smoothly and spend it in exploration of the unknown. Your expertise will be enhanced.

Sometimes in the course of working on a piece, it becomes evident that a miscalculation has been made. You've cut something the wrong size; an accidental slash has been made in the cloth; you've spilled some coffee (or worse) on the working surface, leaving a stain; or some unexpected raveling of cloth edges has happened. It is rare that a piece must be abandoned because of a misadventure. There is usually a way to turn a negative into a positive providing you use ingenuity and do not panic.

During my years of working in fiber, I have had several near-disasters. In almost every case they were salvaged by some fine and fancy improvisation which often resulted in a more interesting work than if the awful thing had not happened.

One which really stands out in my mind is a stitchery hanging done on pale yellow loosely woven material which I had stretched on canvas stretchers, intending to leave it that way for final hanging, just adding a lining on the wrong side. After spending many weeks on the piece I discovered with dismay that the stretcher frame was cutting into the stretched cloth causing the material to split. Something had to be done. I decided to take the work off the stretchers, put filling on the wrong size and cover with cloth to hold it in place, and quilt in the areas which had no stitchery, using the quilting to play up and emphasize the stitchery. Having done that, I lined the back of the piece with the same fabric as the working surface. When the work was finally hung as a soft hanging rather than stretched taut, its overall appearance was a definite improvement; I liked it much better. Here was a case when trouble was a blessing in disguise.

If you inadvertently cut something too small, decide how you can add to the two-small whatever-it-is to fulfill the design requirements. In the case of accidental slits, perhaps the edges of the slits can be worked with a stitch such as buttonhole, leaving the openings as negative spaces in the design. Or you may want to insert something such as a piece of glass, a mirror, a shell, or a pebble in the opening, caging it down and treating the new element just as if it had been planned in the first place! Another thing you can do is to put a contrasting piece of cloth over the slit, appliquéing it and (or) stuffing it from the back, including a spot-stuffed element in the design. Let your imagintion roam; consider all the conceivable options to solve the dilemma. Your "mistakes" can present opportunities to exert your powers of ingenuity and improvisation.

Unexpected raveling of edges is not too difficult to work around. The raveling can be clipped and the raw edge covered with stitchery; or the raveling itself can be exploited as part of the design; or the clipped edge can be turned under and resewn, the only problem then being the reduced size of the raveled piece. If this reduction seriously disturbs the design, consider other alternatives or replace the raveled cloth itself.

Stains from spills onto your work sometimes can be removed with stain remover. If this is impractical, work with the stain, treating it as just another color variation, including it in the design as if it were part of the initial planning. (Only you will know the awful secret!)

A rather heartbreaking miscalculation occurred when I totally covered a T-shirt with patchwork and stitchery, then lined it with calico, finishing it off as meticulously as I could. It pleased me very much when I finally put in the last stitch and rushed to try it on. Alas! I could barely wiggle into it and when I did, it felt like a suit of armor. Then, when trying to take it off, I practically dislocated my shoulders worming my way out of it. What a disaster! And after all that work. What I had not taken into account—and I should have known better—was that the T-shirt upon which all this virtuosity was lavished diminished in size and elasticity as I sewed the patches on, reducing it by at least three sizes by the time it was done. I tried to make it a wearable item by inserting a side zipper, slits in the sleeves and in the bottom of each side, but it still is a most uncomfortable thing to wear. I think it will probably wind up as a soft sculptural form, but for the time being it remains forlornly on its hanger in the clothes closet—a dismal example of not thinking clearly when doing this project. WARNING: When using stretchy T-shirts as working surfaces for patchwork, start out with a *large* T-shirt!

With foresight many miscalculations can be avoided. However, when they do happen don't despair. They can often be made to work for you rather than against you, resulting in more ingenious pieces than you bargained for!

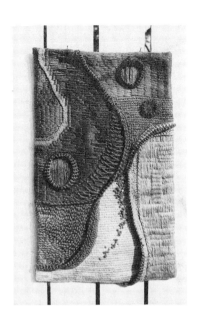

5 Combining Fiber Techniques

Frequent visitors to exhibitions of fiber art are well aware that many of the works shown have utilized several textile procedures in one piece. One sees crocheting used with weaving, combined with stitchery, knitting, or macramé; stuffed forms are often accented with stitchery; woven pieces are sometimes stuffed, even quilted. Any one of the many techniques also frequently stands alone as the only method used to convey an idea. One of the delights of working in fiber is the freedom with which one can approach a problem. No one says "You can't mix these methods in one piece because if you do you will be defying tradition!" Fiber art with its current free, contemporary direction is relatively young compared to the structured rule-laden needle arts which are hundreds of years old and which do have certain traditions, limitations in execution, and rules for excellence. In the freedom of expression as exemplified by the work of today's fiber artists, "rules" are really not an issue. It is expected that whatever one decides to do in creating a work will be done with good craftsmanship, bearing in mind fundamental design principles. But beyond that anything goes—any mixtures of method and materials are valid which, by their use, say what you want to say in the piece. This can be a mixed blessing. One is on safe ground when surrounded by walls of tradition. Concentration can then be placed on excellence of execution rather than on evolving a daring concept. Climbing over those walls is going from the familiar to the unknown and untried; the excitement is not without pitfalls. Consequently, more introspection and ingenuity are required to achieve successful results. Greater effort, however, brings greater satisfaction; the enthusiasm for working in this way is cumulative. It grows on you!

The lines between art and craft are so blurred by now, with hard sculptors experimenting with soft sculpture, painters turning to weaving, potters and ceramacists turning out nonfunctional objects, and stitchers' works taking their place on museum walls, that one is hard put to classify persons working in fiber and the other media formerly considered the province of crafts, as craftspeople. Artist/craftsperson is probably as good a descriptive term as any for those working in media other than painting, hard sculpture, and the graphic arts.

To illustrate this point, I recall an imposing sculptural form shown in an exhibit at the Boston Museum of Fine Arts a few years ago. It was made of heavy dark bronze-black metal in a simple stylized blocklike form which stood about four feet high—as I recall it—on the floor, and gave an impression of massiveness enhanced by a fall of thick dark yarn strands hanging from the top of the piece spilling down onto the floor where they lay in studied disarray. This was an unusual mixture of hard sculpture paired with the softness of fiber.

Whatever size is planned for a piece, whether a grand scale or a smaller, less grandiose presentation, the opportunity exists to include in a single entity several techniques all compatible with the proposed design. The mixture presents a more complex challenge than using just one procedure.

For example, you might plan to make a hanging or form combining stitchery, quilting, and appliqué. When using this combination I've found it easiest to do the appliquéd areas first; they are the large blocks of color. The stitchery can then be put on to harmonize with the appliqué, introducing linear interest. Lastly, the quilting will add surface relief, thus dramatizing both the appliqué and the stitchery. Good design judgment in executing each of these steps should culuminate in a coordinated textile construction.

A couple of years ago, I did a ceiling-hung piece using crochet, stitchery, and stuffed modules. Called *Together We Are One*, it symbolized the peoples of the earth—all races—who, while traveling different paths in the varied locales during their lifetimes, converge together as one—the family of humankind. I crocheted a large, natural-colored jute form with openings into which were put crocheted stuffed modules, each one in the color of one of the races of humans. The next step was doing a stitchery path starting at the top of the form and meandering to each module, then joining at the bottom, to indicate that we are all in this together and not really separate in the larger sense—even though by false notions and prejudice we separate ourselves. To finish off the form I attached several crocheted helixes (long curved strips) to the bottom of the form, wrapping them as a single unit for a couple of inches to further convey the idea of "oneness."

Fig. 5.1 *High Noon*—combination of hooking, stitchery,
folded and clipped felt with hand-made white beads (author).

If the mixture of crochet, stitchery, and stuffing interests you, do try your
own concept using the crocheted form as the nucleus of the design and a
starting point for stitchery. Depending on the shape the form assumes,
decide if stuffing would be appropriate to stabilize the shape. Some yarns
and twines such as jute are so firm when worked that stuffing is not necessary to hold a structure. However when worked with softer, gentler yarns
the form is likely to "go limp" if not bolstered by stuffing. The final touch
is the stitchery which should complement the mood being conveyed.

An important point to consider when using several methods in one project
is the most practical sequence to use when combining. Common sense will
help one to decide which step should be done first. However, sometimes the
idea of adding a technique to a design already in progress is a spontaneous
decision born of the exigencies of the moment. It is not always possible or
desirable to preplan. The traveler who is bound to a schedule is denied the
delights of unplanned side trips. If a flexible attitude toward one's work is
maintained, the options for improvisation are always open. Most times
these spur-of-the-moment changes and additions work out satisfactorily but
they can occasionally lead to awkward situations.

I remember a frustrating experience that occurred after I had made a
patchwork stuffed hanging featuring zippers inserted in some of the patches
which, when opened, revealed different fabrics inside. (The piece was called
The Open and Shut Case.) I decided stitchery was needed for additional interest. The stitchery was done after the stuffing and, because it was done on
the stuffed parts, I kept pulling little bits of filling through to the surface

Fig. 5.2 *The Forest Floor*—hooking, crochet, and stitchery with attached wood bark and crushed velvet (author).

Fig. 5.3 Detail 1 of *The Forest Floor.*

Fig. 5.4 Detail 2 of *The Forest Floor.*

each time I drew the needle in and out. Poking back all those wisps of stuffing really tried my patience! If I had stitched before stuffing no problem would have existed. So if possible, try to forestall situations like this which are so aggravating.

Hooking an element to be part of a design is effective for varying texture. It also gives a relief effect if done in bulky yarns, which when worked, protrude from the working surface. In several pieces I've used hooking combined with puckered or ridged fabric and stitchery. This is a good combination for use in a single piece. One work called *The Forest Floor* (see Figs. 5.2, 5.3, and 5.4) utilized crochet done separately and attached to a piece of rug canvas, one section of which was hooked with the loops left uncut and of varying lengths. Other sections had fabric puckered into crumpled shapes. A small amount of stitchery was used to accent some of the areas. Done with shaggy yarns in shades of greens, browns, and golds, the piece attempted to suggest the floor of the forest. The rough uneven textures seemed appropriate to carry out the theme.

If you are a knitter and have not tried nonfunctional knitting, you might like to experiment with it. Try making flat pieces of knitting in abstract shapes, using small needles if a close texture is desired or large needles if you want a loose, open look. If you use large needles and thin yarn your knitting will look very open and lacy, especially if you vary the tension as you work. I've found carpet thread to be especially nice to work with as well as raffia for a different look. Leave large open spaces in the work, stabilized by closely knitted areas surrounding the negative spaces, switching different sizes of needles as necessary to get desired effects. One can always cast off, then—rejoining the thread to the work—crochet in some of the other areas. You can work in any direction wished or add separate sections, sewing them together. The more one experiments with needle sizes, thread weights,

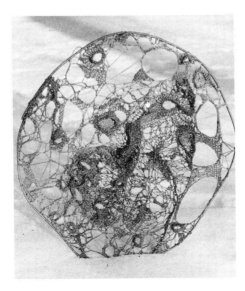

Fig. 5.5 Ceiling-hung knitted and crocheted hanging made with raffia (author).

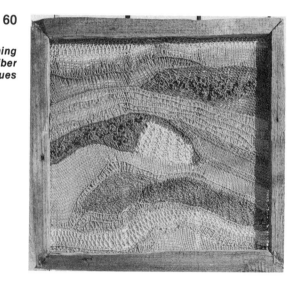

Fig. 5.6 *The Land*—knitted with surface stitchery (author).

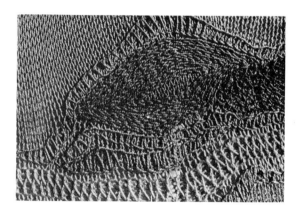

Fig. 5.7 Detail 1 of *The Land.*

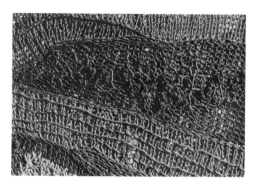

Fig. 5.8 Detail 2 of *The Land.*

tension changes, and direction, the greater the number of variations will occur to you. Ideas seem to spin off each other. Try anything which seems even remotely possible and promising to see what result you get.

Knitting a close, flat surface, stretching it taut on a frame when finished, then stitching on that surface is another combination worthy of investigation (see Figs. 5.6, 5.7, and 5.8). Be sure the knitting is done closely enough to accommodate the stitchery. If the knitting is too loose in texture it will compete with the stitchery, reducing the effectiveness of each. When two or more procedures are combined into a single entity, each method should complement the other but not be competitive. Confusion in design occurs when methods war with one another.

Needle-lace can be a very nice adjunct to a design when combined with fabric. The needle-lace should be done separately and attached later to the fabric on which the design is to be worked. An area of the fabric working surface can be cut away and the needle-lace sewn in the empty space, or the lace can be used directly on the cloth as a focal point from which to plan the balance of the design. The lace can also be a vehicle to cage in objects such as glass, shells, pebbles, marbles, and mirrors. When you use needle-lace in a negative space the cast shadows from it—if the finished piece is hung a few inches away from the wall—provide an additional design factor.

The generally structured technique of needlepoint can be used to create abstract designs with a freer, more spontaneous appearance than the usual results of this method. Working on rug canvas with heavy yarns I've found that one can successfully execute flowing, curving abstract designs quite removed from the ordinary flora and fauna one usually sees done in needlepoint. Unlike the other fiber procedures discussed in this chapter, the use of needlepoint necessitates some preplanning because of certain constrictions inherent in working on rug canvas with its evenly placed holes. One must take these constrictions into account when working out a design plan. Needlepoint combined with stitchery and crochet can result in original and unusual fiber designs (see Figs. 5.9 and 5.10). The needlepoint surface

Figs. 5.9, 5.10 (Left) *The Three Circles*— free, unstructured needlepoint with surface stitchery crochet (author). (Below) Detail of *The Three Circles.*

Fig. 5.11 Macramé wall-piece with stuffed element (author).

Fig. 5.12 Detail of macramé wall-piece showing stuffed element.

is done first, of course, and then the color blocks are augmented with top stitchery and crochet, using the latter to give surface relief to the two-dimensional surface. The crochet, standing away from the needlepoint surface casts shadows which add depth to the design, enhancing it.

Macramé, which has become almost a household word among craft-oriented people, can readily be one of the components of technique combinations. It lends form, shape, and body to both two- and three-dimensional designs. One mixture I've tried and liked was used in a primarily knotted (macraméd) hanging combined with stuffed fabric-covered elements (see Figs. 5.11 and 5.12). The piece, although mostly two-dimensional, had depth in the stuffed sections—a nice contrast. As the final step in the work process the stuffed parts were added to the open spaces in the macramé. When doing macramé it is wise to avoid overdoing when adding elements. The knotted surface is rich in texture and contour; if anything else is included it should serve as visual relief from the liveliness of the knotting rather than compete with it. The smooth fabric-covered stuffed shapes performed that function without complication or busyness.

In the amalgam of two or more techniques in one piece one should bear in mind the following tips to create a smoother working course, culminating in successful resolution of the design.

62   As mentioned previously in this chapter, try if possible to anticipate the sequence of working steps to avoid unnecessary aggravation. This does not preclude spontaneity in development of ideas; as one experiments one gets to know the characteristics of the various fiber methods and what the difficulties are in each. Work is planned accordingly. If a superb inspiration comes to you after the piece is begun, even if it is difficult to implement that inspiration, try. You will learn then if it is just difficult or downright impossible! (A valuable lesson for future reference.)

When quilting, use threads which are easily drawn in and out of a fabric and wax them for additional strength. It's annoying to have threads breaking frequently.

If you choose appliqué for a design element, consider the mood of your piece as well as its projected use when you decide how to sew it down. Raw edges can be very lovely with their gently fraying and loose, straying threads—but not on functional items. With wear and laundering those raw edges may fray out of existence!

Crochet is very versatile and all its ramifications should be explored so you will become familiar with the variations in appearance you can achieve by experimentation. Try switching hook sizes and yarn weights in one piece to create spatially open to contrastingly dense, heavy looks—intriguing interplay. Crochet several weights and colors of yarn together to observe what happens to the colors and textures.

Figs. 5.13, 5.14 (Left) Stuffed, quilted, and stitched wall-piece (author). (Right) Detail of stuffed, quilted, and stitched wall-piece.

When stuffing elements, one can use rags, old discarded panty hose, socks, and stockings as filler material as well as bagged commercial filler. Before buying stuffing supplies, check around the house to see if you can improvise with discards to serve your purpose.

Remember to do the stitchery first (if possible) if you plan to use it on stuffed sections. If the stitchery is an afterthought a curved needle is useful; use as small a one as will accommodate the thread, to keep to a minimum drawing little bits of filling through to the surface as you stitch. They can—as I mentioned previously—be poked back in, but it's a nuisance.

Knitting tends to collapse back on itself and doesn't hold a shape unless done with heavy cotton yarn, twine, or rope. To give it body and to retain contours, block it when finished. While it is stretched out and pinned in place to block, spray it with a heavy solution of liquid starch, letting it dry thoroughly. The knitted piece can also be wired on the wrong side, the wire sewn carefully with matching thread. Another alternative is to weight it top and bottom with something heavy of suitable size. The top edge can be attached to a rod or, if weighted with individual heavy objects, that edge can be hung over the rod to hang down in back for an inch or so, secured with a few stitches to prevent its slipping off the rod. Bottom weights can be beads, fish sinkers, washers, nuts or bolts, caged pebbles, marbles or shells, by-the-yard dress hem weighting, spools, or whatever else you can think of. The piece can be tacked to a frame or, if a less formal look is indicated, attached to a tree branch. The lighter-weight threads and yarns need more stabilization, as one might expect. Whatever method you use to present the knitted design should be carefully considered for appropriateness to complement the work and show it off to its best advantage.

When working up a piece in macramé, use heavier cords if you are a beginner. It is much easier to see what is going on in the knotting process if the cord is of heavy yarn or twine than with the finer threads. When the process is thoroughly familiar, do try some of the thinner threads to compare effects. Carpet thread (the old-fashioned kind) is very nice when knotted giving a crisp look to the work. Perle cotton, weaving yarns, and crochet cotton also look effective when knotted.

Avoid using too many techniques in one work. Just as the use of too varied a selection of stitches in a single piece muddies the waters, so too will a multitude of methods. At the same time be daring, innovative, and unafraid to try the unusual and to develop sensitivity in interpretation of ideas.

Most of all, enjoy what you are doing—your work will reflect your attitude.

The Third Dimension -Soft Sculpture and Relief

6

In the 1960s three-dimensional fiber forms began to appear in exhibitions and gallery showings. Although initially referred to as forms or objects, the terms "soft sculpture" or "fiber sculpture" became accepted definitions for three-dimensional fiber statements.

An article by Mimi Shorr, entitled "Fiber Sculpture," which appeared in the May 20, 1972, issue of *Saturday Review*, dealt with the impact of fiber form upon the art world. Many artists were mentioned in the article as having early contributed significant and authoritative works achieving legitimate status in the art world. Lenore Tawney, Claire Zeisler, Sheila Hicks, Olga de Amaral, Magda Abakanowicz, Jagoda Buic, Francoise Grossen, Moik Schiele, and Ed Rossbach—all played an important part in the evolution of fiber sculpture, inspiring other artists to become part of the vanguard of a new movement.

Many artists, excited by the possibilities inherent in the use of fiber for development of design concepts, began to create works which startled, astonished, disquieted, sometimes amused, and many times confounded viewers. Claes Oldenburg, with his environmental works and fiber interpretations of everyday objects, inspired many fiber artists to express themselves in form rather than two-dimensionally.

Fig. 6.1 *The Shattered Heart*—stuffed modules, crumpled velvet, crochet (author).

Fig. 6.2 Detail of *The Shattered Heart.*

Currently, we expect to see form in fiber shows and it would be a rare show indeed which excluded the third dimension. Stuffed forms, shaped weaving, sculptural macramé, coiled objects, crocheted shapes—all types of fiber manipulation are used to convey an idea in form. All this ferment provides the experimenter with a fertile field upon which to explore ideas and new materials. Nothing which works is too extreme; nothing violates any rules because there are no rules to break—an exhilarating state of affairs for the artist! This heady atmosphere provides a peculiar challenge. Sometimes it is difficult to come down to earth and settle on specifics when developing a fiber design. So many options churn around in one's mind that the possibilities seem infinite. As has been previously mentioned, it is well to reinforce the notion of simplicity and avoid too much variety in any one work thus risking incoherence in that work.

Among the many methods of forming shapes, stuffing is one of the simplest. One can work spontaneously letting the piece evolve as successive steps are taken, or a careful sketch can be made before actual work is begun. If you preplan the design, you might want to cut out paper patterns, stuff them with crumpled tissue or newspaper, and staple or tape them as a rough mock-up to see if the design is corresponding satisfactorily to the sketch.

66 The mock-up can be readjusted or amended until it correctly interprets the design. Then the cloth can be cut and stuffed without costly or time-consuming error and with reasonable assurance that the idea will be expressed as it is envisioned.

It may take a bit of practice, learning to visualize from the sketch the shapes to be cut, to carry out the concept. Experiment with simple design ideas at first, cutting newspaper to make patterns which can be easily manipulated, assembled, and thrown away after they've served the purpose. Initial attempts worked out in paper help to avoid failures in the later fabric project.

The materials one uses for stuffing can be many different things. Polyester or dacron filler, crumpled paper tissue, old stockings or panty hose, rags, plastic foam, polystyrene pellets, straw, recycled pillow innards—anything you can think of which will do the job aesthetically and economically. Clearly if one has a huge form to fill, cost is an important factor and efforts should be made to use discards wherever possible. It always surprises me to see what people throw away; it gives a measure of satisfaction to be able to resurrect some of these tossed-aside materials, especially in the light of heightened ecological awareness. Avoid wasting materials throughtlessly. Yesterday's throwaway may be today's perfect medium.

Letting a sculptural design grow step by step and making decisions as work progresses gives one a good deal of creative latitude. Without preconceived design specifications one is free to amend the work at each stage of development. Many fiber artists prefer this method of working. Once a piece is underway the gradually evolving appearance will sometimes suggest a mood which can then be exploited by shaping, choice of materials, and type of technique to bring it to fruition.

If the step-by-step way of creating is appealing, a starting point can be a simple form, either cut from cloth to be stuffed, or crocheted, knotted, or

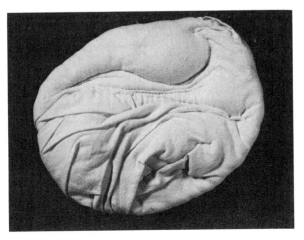

Fig. 6.3 Quilted, stuffed, and manipulated fiber form (Betsy Cannon).

Fig. 6.4 *Nostalgia*—knitted
construction on tree branch with shells
(Anita Leutwiler; photograph courtesy
of the artist).

coiled, with the result analyzed to see what it suggests. Sometimes nothing!
But a good form, even if not specifically evocative, is worth working for its
own sake. (I always suspect this is the case when a work is named *Untitled* or
Form #1, etc., at showings!) It is well to remember that a sculptural form
must be artistically valid from all viewing sides, with no discernible "front"
or "back."

Of course you may be working with an existing hanging which would be
improved by adding three-dimensional interest. In that case, putting a protruding element on a flat surface would be considered low relief rather than
sculpture, with the relief attained by quilting, wiring, stuffing, crocheting,
etc. If quilting or stuffing is used, a piece of cloth must be used under the
working surface to hold the filling in place (see Chapter 6).

A nice linear effect can be had by stitching parallel lines on the working
surface (using a piece of cloth underneath as in quilting and stuffing) and
running cord through the resulting "tunnel," using a bodkin or a safety pin
attached to the cord as a pushing tool. The tool used to get the cord through
the tunnel depends on the width of the tunnel. Although I haven't tried the
following procedure, I would think one could lay the cord underneath the
working surface and, holding it in place with another piece of cloth as in
stuffing and quilting, baste all three together in place. Then hand-stitch on
either side along the cord's length, raising it above the surface. It would
seem that if you wanted to get a complex curving corded design, it would be
easier to do it this way rather than stitching first, then trying to thread the
cord through all those twisting channels.

Pockets or pouches, either crocheted or made with separate pieces of
fabric, can be made on the top side of the working surface or underneath it.
These can be stuffed with the open side sewn down afterward; or perhaps

one might leave the open side as is, with a fall of yarns spilling out of the pocket. There are many little improvisations one will be led to try, motivated by the circumstances prevailing at the moment.

The crocheted forms one sees in current exhibitions are light years removed from the doilies, dresser scarves, handkerchief edgings, and so on which were the products of our grandmothers' busy hands. Crochet is ideally suited as a form- and texture-giving technique and is widely used by today's fiber artists to create both two- and three-dimensional works. The possibilities for unusual effects are almost unlimited. Because of this versatility crochet has become one of the most valuable methods in the designer's repertoire.

One way to begin developing a form using crochet is to chain a line about 10 to 12 inches long and single crochet back and forth for a few rows until you have a strip which is sizeable enough to hold and to work with easily. Then put your hook in the strip randomly, chaining a line tangentially from the original strip. Crochet back and forth along your new line for a few rows, then hook back into the original strip and work along the irregular edge. Do this several times in different directions, crocheting along the forming edges. You will readily see how the shape is beginning to evolve. Then crochet almost anywhere in the embryonic sculpture, emphasizing openings, curves, and undulations at will. Decrease (inserting the hook into two openings instead of one then crocheting one stitch) or increase (crochet two stitches into one opening) stitches to change the form's structure. If you have openings in your piece, you might want to insert some stuffing as you go along to firm and stabilize selective areas. If, however, the crochet is done with sisal (see Figs. 6.5 and 6.6) or jute this is hardly ever necessary because of the firmness of these materials when crocheted. Although this process of form developing might sound a bit puzzling, once you have tried

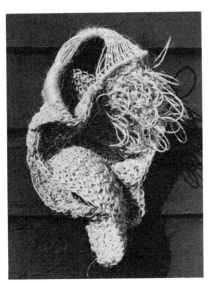

Fig. 6.5 Crocheted sisal form— view 1 (author).

Fig. 6.6 Crocheted sisal form—view 2.

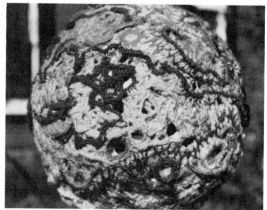

Fig. 6.8 Detail of crochet-covered ball.

Fig. 6.7 Crochet-covered ball with stitchery (author).

it the rapid evolution of the form as it is worked will demonstrate clearly how crocheting in this manner works.

One can start a form in crochet in other ways besides the one just described. Rounds can be made, stuffed, and formed into modules which can be attached to one another, thus building a single entity. Basketlike forms can be made; crocheted strips can be linked ringlike and sewn to form any kind of shape, roundish or longish. Crocheting can be done along the edges of these rings forming deep openings which can be filled with modules. As a form grows, solutions to the problems it poses as each new element is added will occur to the experimenter, resulting in fresh and original approaches to the third dimension.

Relief and textured surfaces add depth and interest to many hangings, and can be the primary components of wall-pieces. Crocheting a surface of uneven height by varying the crochet stitch from single to double or treble, by crocheting back and forth in selected sections, or by yarning over the bars created by the double and treble crochet are ways of developing relief. Increasing and decreasing stitches in rows will pucker or ruffle the surface and provide opportunities for stuffing or wiring from underneath. Crocheting with ridges (see Chapter 3, the section on crocheting) will give linear emphasis. Here, too, it is likely that you will soon try your own variations **70** when exploring the possibilities of crocheted relief.

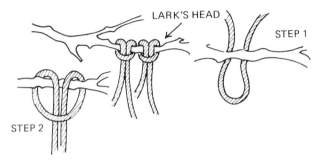
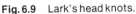

Fig. 6.9   Lark's head knots.

Fig. 6.10   Double half-hitch knot.

Knotting is another form-giving possibility. One can attach cords to tree branches, rings, wire amatures, or anything else you might think of to which cords might be attached. The cords are easily fastened by a lark's head (see Fig. 6.9) and then worked in whatever kind of knotting is most effective for the purpose. The double half-hitch (see Fig. 6.10) is a good stabilizing knot for a beginning piece and is also versatile enough so that entire pieces can be worked in half-hitch alone with very effective results. Square knots (see Chapter 3, the section on knots), half-square knots, or any way you choose to knot the cords—all will work out for in-the-round, as well as two-dimensional forms. Knotting is also an excellent way to deal with the loose ends with which one is sometimes confronted when using other techniques; it is a nice addition to sculptures primarily formed by another method, but which could benefit by the addition of a contrasting manipulation. There are many excellent books dealing specifically with design using knotting. If this particular method interests you, it is suggested that the Bibliography be consulted for further reference. You will soon learn that the possibilities using this technique are enormous.

Braids are also a simple but effective way of building a sculpture. One can start with a single braid, knot or coil that braid, make another braid, and attach it (by sewing or tying—even wiring) to the first braid, and so on, developing the form bit by bit until it is in the mind of its creator completed.

Regardless of the methods you use for working up a soft sculpture, check its development from all angles as it progresses to ascertain its validity from each viewing angle.

A challenging way to develop a form in-the-round is to work in a tangle, crocheting, knotting, braiding, or wrapping into, around, and from the twisted mass of cords, yarn, rope, or whatever makes up the tangle. We frequently have odds and ends of threads, yarn, string, or even wire that wind up in a hopeless mess, impossible to straighten and separate. This mass of twisted material can be the nucleus of a cohesive form when you use the snarl as part of a larger composition. One can attach additional cords to some of the tangled cords and braid, knot, or wrap them with yarns which are compatible with the material in the tangle. Choose colors and textures

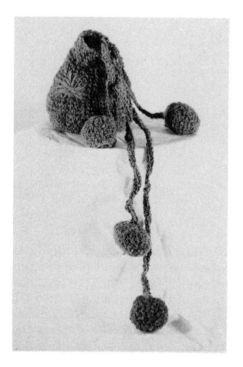

Fig. 6.12 Soft sculptural form (author).

Fig. 6.11 Soft sculptural form—stitchery accent (author).

for the working yarns which carry out the feeling generated by the mass (mess?) you are working with.

Or you might consider using yarns diametrically opposed in feeling with the snarled nucleous—a departure from the obvious. For instance, the apparent incongruity of a weathered, rustic snarl of rope wrapped in elegant silky threads or plushy voluptous chenille yarn may make the point you have in mind. Unusual surprises in a piece can be delightful if they are done in such a way as to indicate a tongue-in-cheek deliberate choice, not simply poor judgment. Conveying *that* mastery over materials is a challenge to the ingenuity of the artist! Can one make a silk purse out of a sow's ear? Well, literally, of course not, but figuratively? It's worth some consideration. One should not be so deadly serious when working that an artistic joke is out of the question. Wit and humor in fiber statements, as in life itself, are the leavening which lighten our burdens and make bearable the unbearable.

Crocheted elements such as modules, sections of looping (check the Bibliography for books on crochet stitches), and long helixes can be attached to the snarl after being made separately. You could also use one of the snarled cords from the tangle as a foundation for crocheting swatches that can be sewn to the tangle itself. It's really fun to be involved in bringing about the metamorphosis of a mess to a valid sculptural statement.

72 Of course stuffed, fabric-covered shapes as well as found objects can be added to the snarl, depending from cords and hanging down, tucked into apertures, or sewn to the outside of the tangle—anything you can imagine to include them as integral parts of the total form.

When working in the round, the end results are sometimes best displayed as ceiling-hung pieces so they can be viewed from all angles. If, however you wish the piece to be virtually free-standing or lying horizontally on a surface—even the floor—consideration must be given to firmness so the object won't collapse limply or tip to one side. Lying horizontally on a surface isn't quite so demanding and in fact, you might design to include limp sections to contrast with the firm structures. I have a jute free-standing piece made several years ago, which is always listing to one side and which is conscientiously straightened each time I pass it—the result of poor planning in the amount of interior stuffing it received. Bear in mind what the final presentation of the piece is to be and adjust the construction accordingly.

To eliminate worry over the firmness of your soft sculpture, an armature of wire can be made to work over. The armature can be made of screening, chicken wire, or any easily bent wire which can be shaped to support the shell which will encase it. Even a sturdy tree branch can serve as interior stabilization. The armature itself can be part of the design, leaving some of it exposed. One year I decided to crochet a tree form in shades of greens to serve as a Christmas tree. The idea was practical enough but instead of using wire for the armature, I used a cardboard tube, with tree branches inserted at intervals over which to crochet. Although the form stood upright, it was too blocky and tippy with the branches proving too fragile to support the crochet, thus breaking and spoiling the shape.

Fig. 6.13 *Evolving Form*—soft form crocheted with white cord, with fabric-covered modules; base crocheted of soft, hairy yarn (author).

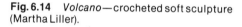
Fig. 6.14 *Volcano*—crocheted soft sculpture (Martha Liller).

Fig. 6.15 Detail of *Volcano*.

One can, however, learn from one's failures. When an idea seems basically sound, it is good discipline to redo it if the first attempt at realization is less than ideal. The second time around the bugs can be ironed out, with success more predictable.

Basketry techniques are currently being used more and more for the resolution of fiber ideas. Some inspiring pieces have been shown, illustrating to what lengths an old technique can be carried in the hands of contemporary artists. A work which comes to mind was shown at "Fiberworks," City Hall, Boston, Massachusetts, in 1975. This basketry wall-piece, entitled *Burden Basket* was done in earth-colored rawhide and sticks, with a leather face worked deep within the bowl-shaped form. Utilizing an ancient method, the artist, Marcia Floor, created a strong compelling statement which impressed me deeply.

In a new and exciting book called *Textile Techniques in Metal,* by Arline Fisch, there is a photograph of an intriguing coiled basket done in sterling silver wire. (Directions for the coiling procedure will be discussed in Chapter 10.)

Observing and analyzing the three-dimensional pieces made with the coiling technique, it is clear that this method is not only exciting in its possibilities but easy and versatile to use in the development of sculptural forms. Shapes and wrapping materials can be readily changed as the piece progresses, giving wide latitude in designing while a fascinating entity emerges before your eyes. Coiling, as with other methods, is amenable to mixture with other techniques but it is interesting enough in its own right to be the sole design element. The results as one changes direction, curves back on previously worked sections, and adjusts the design to allow for intervening negative spaces, are a continual surprise and allow ample opportunity for spontaneous decision-making.

After checking the basic directions for the coiling process, begin a piece by coiling an area large enough to hold easily. The first few inches are the most awkward because you don't have enough done and in hand to grasp easily. However, persist until the completed section is at least roughly 2 inches in diameter. Then the whole process becomes simple and attention can be paid to the development of the design. Try an abstract, meandering course in the coiling (see Fig. 6.18), leaving empty (negative) spaces, then converging at a point further on to reattach the core that is being wrapped and coiled. Having become aware of the options available in coiling, you are free to go off in any direction desired, whether it be a completely abstract three-dimensional form, a wall piece done in relief, a functional basket-form, or whatever fancy dictates. A piece I finished recently has two cuplike openings included in a primarily enclosed abstract shape. Into these two

Fig. 6.16 Wall-piece of spool-knitted tubing, stuffed and crocheted (author).

Fig. 6.17 Detail of wall-piece.

Fig. 6.18 Abstract coiling pattern, rejoining coiling at irregular intervals.

Fig. 6.19 Abstract coiled form with two openings into which plants are inserted (author).

openings I inserted two small plants, one of baby tears, the other a spreading artillary plant (see Fig. 6.19). It's a pretty different sort of planter!

Fabrics such as burlap, monk's cloth or similar loosely woven materials can be manipulated into three-dimensional forms by pulling threads and gathering up the cloth as the threads are pulled. A satisfactory experiment can be performed with a yard of burlap by pulling the threads randomly and sewing the resulting gathers in place to secure the form. Study the effect as this is done in several places on the cloth, sewing edges and folds together where necessary to retain the shape. Gathering can also be done by sewing lines of stitches and then pullng up the stitches to form gathers, bearing in mind that you are striving for a three-dimensional object. Stuff the form if it seems limp, inserting the stuffing as you go along. Burlap is so crisp, however, that shapes are easily held without stuffing.

When the overall shape seems interesting enough to consider the fabric manipulation step finished, analyze it to see if the addition of other design elements would be an improvement or a distraction from an entity already valid in its own right. Don't decorate for the sake of adding something. Many a lovely shape has been rendered busy and trivial by the addition of unnecessary components. But if the piece cries out for accents, for dramatization, for focus, give careful consideration to what could be done to resolve the situation. Sometimes crocheting along a curve accenting that curve is a good solution. Or perhaps some stitchery meandering over some of the surfaces will unify the piece and provide proper focus. Knotted or

76 braided elements, the incorporation of found objects—all sorts of options exist to help bring a work to its full realization. Bring thoughtfulness, a flexible mind, and a daring spirit to your work; you and it will profit accordingly. Exploring the third dimension is another avenue of experimentation for the fiber designer and one which presents its own unique problems and its own special rewards.

7 Practical Things to Make

Fiber art can and does include the practical as well as the nonfunctional object. Some of the useful creations turned out by contemporary fiber artists are so ingenious in concept, so sensitive in use of materials, so daringly interpreted that they deserve and get their rightful place for display when not in use. Paraphernalia of everyday use have been transformed from the ordinary to the unique by the lively minds, creative wit, and virtuosity of those working in this genre. Such transformation has resulted in garments, body ornaments, jewelry, quilts, toys—all sorts of things—which boggle the mind with the fantasy, whimsy, and satire of their designing. They provoke reaction, sometimes positive, sometimes negative, rarely indifferent!

Many people enjoy making primarily useful things rather than creating the nonfunctional object. The opportunities for resolving fresh, original, useful fiber ideas are only as limited as one's imagination; they can be just as inspiring as those for developing the nonfunctional statement. It is also a refreshing change of pace to make something one can use—wall space runs out after awhile! And think of the gift-giving possibilities. A personally created gift includes a part of the creator, and thus is meaningful and likely to be treasured by the recipient. Selfishly speaking, one can get much personal pleasure from giving away those things upon which time, love, and knowledge have been expended.

PILLOW DESIGNS

These days, the pillow has become an object of almost endless variety. Ranging in size from tiny baby pillows to great pillows serving as beds, the pillow has been exploited far beyond its conventional use of a few years past. Wall pillows—really wall sculptures—that can be removed from the wall to serve a more practical function; bean bag chairs and settees that are really giant squashy pillows which invitingly envelope the body when one curls up in them; large floor cushions that can replace formal chairs in more casual room environments; elegant accent pillows that give spice to living areas; and enchanting, imaginative children's pillows—all these pillow forms have engaged the creative interest of fiber artists. Unusual materials and unconventional color schemes have played their part toward the further development of contemporary pillow forms.

When designing pillows decide upon the obvious factors first—size, function, projected setting, whether for adult or child, and any other specifications such as future wear and tear, washability, or other type of cleaning process necessary for upkeep. These factors will determine the type of yarn, fabric, and other materials required for the design resolution. Consider materials such as fur scraps, plastic by-the-yard, and leather as well as fabrics when working out the idea. A pillow upon which you rest bare skin should be tactilely pleasant. This might preclude the use of leather or plastic if their surfaces feel unpleasant against the skin. Durability is a must, especially for any child's pillow which is likely to undergo considerable stress and strain.

The basic method for putting the pillow together is the same whatever technique is used; the first step is to construct an "envelope" which you will stuff to form the pillow. The envelope can be a large piece of material doubled over with the two open sides sewn together, or two separate pieces of fabric sewn together on three sides (on the wrong side) and turned inside out so the seaming is on the inside. If you wish to cover a raw seam with binding, ribbon, or some other trimming, then the pieces can be seamed on the right sides. Although inner pillow forms can be bought they are so perfectly shaped as to be rather uninteresting. The bagged filler one uses for quilting is, to me, preferable. It allows for those little irregular edges which are so much more appealing.

Everywhere these days it seems one is encountering patchwork. Many of the updated versions of early American folk art are fashionable and very attractive. Pillows with patchwork motifs or entirely patched are simple to make and practically explain themselves if you look at them closely. If your tastes lean away from the traditional toward the contemporary, you can make stunning patchwork using the very modern materials from Finland and other similar fabrics. Patches can be cut in abstract shapes and sewn together, departing from the usual geometric approach. A patchwork motif appliquéd to a fabric can serve as a pillow top. Patching the entire top is another option. You may wish to work out an appliquéd abstract—or representational—design for the pillow, to which stitchery can be added if

79 desired.

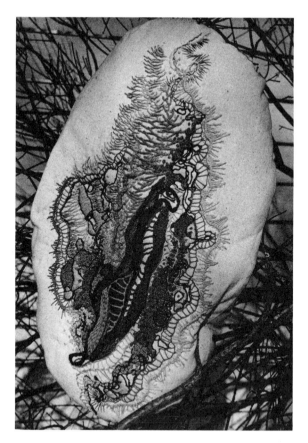

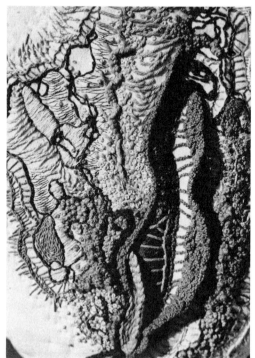

Fig. 7.2 Detail of oval pillow.

Fig. 7.1 Oval pillow—extensive use of stitchery (author).

A word of caution: make the pillow-top design *before* sewing up the envelope. If the envelope is made first, then working on the top part is much more awkward.

One of the most unconventional pillows I ever made was inspired by a contemporary printed cloth with large black dots and long black, orange, and pink stripes. I gathered the cloth in an irregular shape, puckered the dots wth a gathering thread, and also put other gathering threads here and there to further distort the overall shape. Appliquéd pieces of other fabrics that complemented the primary cloth were added along with stitchery. This odd shape was finally stuffed and named *Pillow Gone Mad* (see Figs. 7.3 and 7.4). It looked as if it had! But I like it.

Old pillows, no longer attractive, can serve as bases on which to sew new materials, to crochet over, or to become the innards of a whole new top.

Consider using offbeat materials such as mirrors, beads, lace, roving, unspun wool, braids when making your pillows. Use of unusual additions to pillows will transform them from the pedestrian to the unique.

Fig. 7.3 *Pillow Gone Mad*—gathered fabric, appliquéd with stitchery (author).

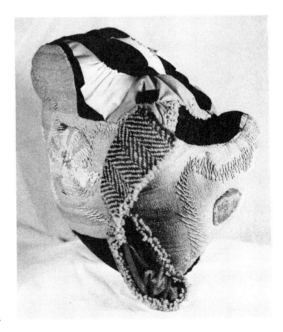

Fig. 7.4 *Pillow Gone Mad*—view 2.

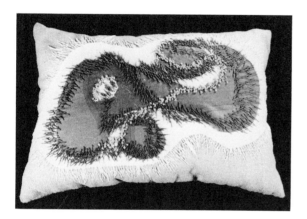

Fig. 7.5 Pillow with appliqué and stitchery (author).

Fig. 7.6 Crocheted pillow (author).

Crochet, weaving, knitting, and knotting are all possible options for use in making pillows. If the pillow is to be really used and not a "show but not to blow" type, consideration should be given to tactile appeal, ease of upkeep, and durability.

Crochet can be used to make motifs to put on fabrics, or crochet itself can be the single process used for the pillow (see Fig. 7.6). Try crocheting irregular roundish areas or perhaps rectangular shapes, varying the width within each rectangle and crocheting them together as you go along. You can build a very abstract design, letting it grow as new parts are added. Stop when it seems a reasonable size—and "reasonable" means many things to many people! So your pillow may be a very small accent or a huge contained "environment," itself an invitation to fold oneself within its depths.

82

Stitchery is very effective done on top of a crocheted surface. It should be limited, though, in the number of different stitches in one piece. Otherwise it might look confused when combined with a crocheted background. I've tried using one stitch only—a squared chain—meandering it all over a crimson crocheted background, using closely related shades of reds and red-oranges for the stitchery (see Fig. 7.7). It seemed to work well.

Be sure to spray your finished pillows (and all your fiber work) with a dirt and moisture repellent. Your pieces will stay bright and clean-looking for years, needing only to be vacuumed with the dusting attachment to retain their initial freshness.

BAG DESIGNS

Heralded by the skirl of bagpipes, the exhibition "Homage to the Bag" opened at the Museum of Contemporary Crafts, New York City, on October 10, 1975, and continued until January 4, 1976. Dedicated to an object used by man for hundreds of years, the show featured bags ranging from contemporary designs by artists and craftspeople to those of primitive cultures as well as the professional, sports, travel, disposable, and storage bags of everyday living. Think of all the types of bags one uses all the time: handbags, tea bags, sleeping bags, shoe bags, musette bags, knapsacks—the list can go on and on. Consider the infinite variety of the bag, the ingenuity required in the designing and assembling of the different types, all geared

83

toward their own special function. *Crafts Horizons,* October 1975, carries on its cover a handsome hand-built clay bag (clearly not intended for use!) entitled *Hanging Canvas and Leather Bag,* executed by Marilyn Levine, which was shown in "Homage to the Bag." Also in this issue is an excellent series of photographs of some of the bags on view in "Homage to the Bag"; the photographs give a sampling of the range and variety of bags in terms of function, design, and materials used.

In the past few years bags have assumed a special prominence in our life styles. Many young people travel great distances carrying their belongings stuffed in bags, some in back-pack style with many zippered compartments, others simply slung over their shoulders sailor-style. The informality of the bag has made it attractive even to some older people (although I suspect the numbers of oldsters going through the luggage inspection line at Kennedy International with a duffle bag slung over their shoulders are few). New parents carry their offspring in uniquely styled bag-type slings and baglike back packs, a belated recognition of something the Indians knew when this country was in its infancy.

Bags are fun to make, practical to use, and provide much opportunity for originality in design.

A crocheted bag works up very quickly. Try crocheting abstract shapes in a coordinated color scheme. When changing colors try crocheting together both the new color yarn and the color you are changing from. The transition from one color to another will be more subtle if you blend this way for a few rows before using the new color by itself.

Another idea that I've used with crochet is to make tubing with an old-fashioned knitting spool—a spool with four or more pegs equally spaced, protuding about ½ inch from one end of the spool. This little tool, sold in most ten-cent stores, and often used by children who make potholders out of the tubing, is now made mostly in plastic (naturally!) but one can easily make one's own. I have one with eight finishing nails set around one end of large hollow wood cylinder; this makes wider tubing which can be stuffed. Directions for use come with the purchased knitting spools, and can also be found in *The Textile Arts,* by Verla Birrell, pp. 300-302. They are very easy to use and the tubing is great for couching down on working surfaces in interesting linear designs, giving a three-dimensional look to that surface. A bag I made in three shades of denim blue involves a crocheted basic bag shape with additional surface crochet standing away from it and couched down knitted tubing. The design also had a portion of one side done in loop stitch, the shaggy loops delineating one edge and giving it an asymetrical appearance.

A good way to use up worn-out turkish towels is to use the towel as a base upon which to sew patches of preferably irregular shapes (the structured geometric patterns are much more conventional and thus less amenable to imaginative interpretation), then apply stitchery on the patched surface. One bag made while I was glued to the televised Senate Select Committee's hearings on Watergate—and which kept my hands busy and my nerves intact during the unfolding of the drama—was constructed in just this way,

Banner—detail (Fredrica Galley;
photo courtesy of the artist)

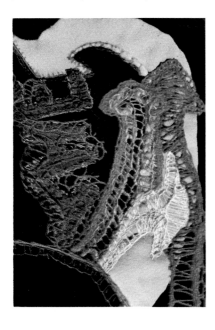

Yellow fiber construction
(Anita Leutwiler; photo courtesy
of the artist)

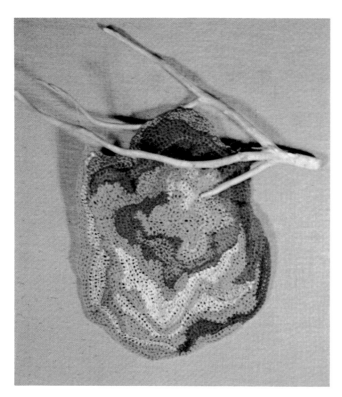

Renaissance (author)

Sea Pattern (author)

Knotless netting (Fredrica Galley; photo courtesy of the artist)

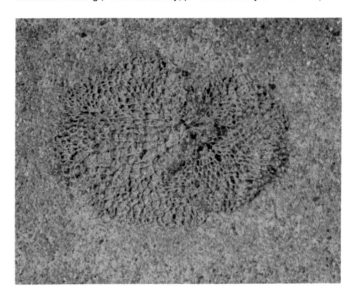

Study in Red-Two (author)

Yellow Tracery (author)

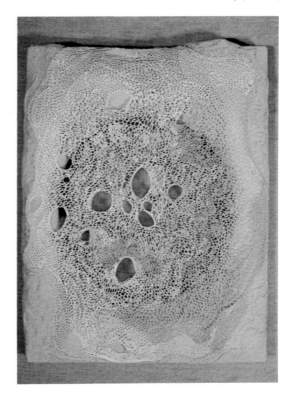

Banner (Fredrica Galley; photo courtesy of the artist)

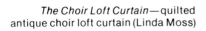

Crocheted wallpiece (Catherine Wilder)

The Choir Loft Curtain—quilted
antique choir loft curtain (Linda Moss)

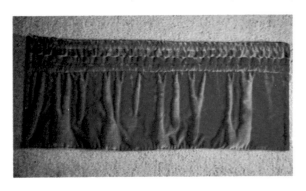

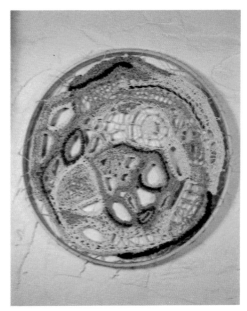

Levels—crocheted with appliquéd inner layer (author)

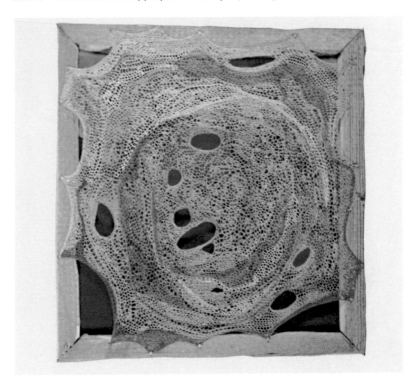

The Weaver's Workshop—stitchery
(Linda Moss)

Crocheted bag (Anita Leutwiler;
photo courtesy of the artist)

Reverse appliqué—work in progress
(Linda Moss)

Untitled—stitchery (Martha Liller)

Tangle (author)

Sunburst—coiled wallpiece
with braids (author)

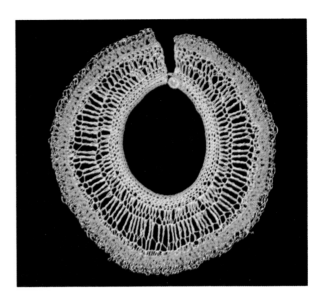

Necklace—crocheted kite string,
squid line, and gilt thread (author)

Memoir—crocheted hanging
with stitchery (author)

Pillow—stitchery on crocheted
surface (author)

Pillow Gone Mad—stuffed form
with stitchery (author)

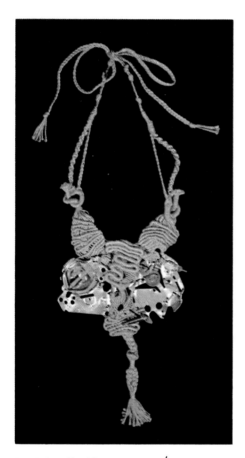

Wallpiece—spontaneous macramé
(author)

Clock Part Necklace—macramé with
crushed clock parts (author)

Door banner—quilted felt (Betsy Cannon)

Stitchery—unfinished (Osa Segal)

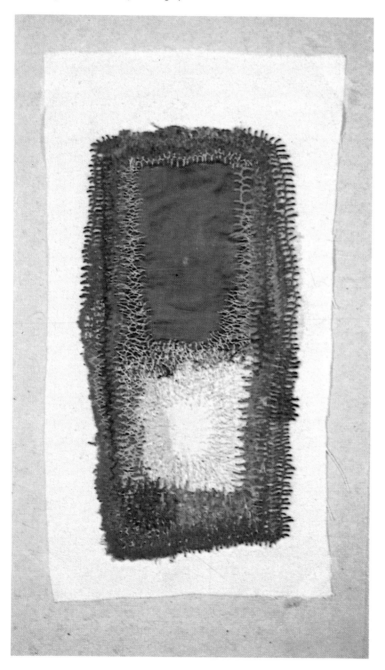

Watergate Bag—appliquéd with
stitchery—view 1 (author)

Watergate Bag—view 2

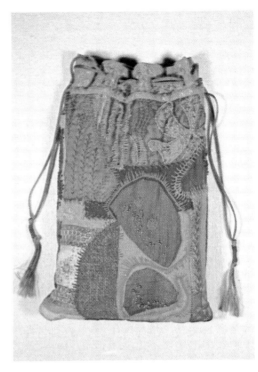

Stitchery (Martha Liller)

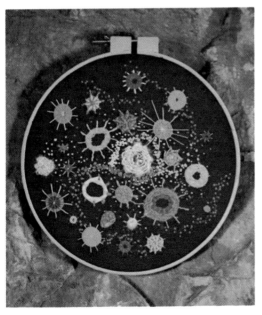

Campobello—collage
of beach stones, found ropes,
and twines (Catherine Wilder)

Chrysalis—detail (Harriett L. Morrison)

Fig. 7.8 *Watergate Bag*—patchwork with stitchery (author).

Fig. 7.9 *Watergate Bag*—view 2.

starting with an old towel worn thin. The patches used were pretty wools, silks, and brocades, some in muted colors and rather Victorian in feeling (see Figs. 7.8 and 7.9). The stitchery was done freely, wandering all over the patched surface, disregarding edges of the individual patches. In some areas I sewed on small gold beads which looked, after being sewn, as if they had just fallen on the bag. Small holes edged with buttonhole stitch were made along the top edge of the bag to accommodate the drawstring which was made of silky parachute cord. The ends of the drawstring were yarn wrapped both for interest and to prevent raveling. This bag carries special meaning for me, made as it was during the traumatic revelations of a dark period in our nation's history.

Another bag with considerably less momentous connotations is one which was once a shoe bag with a drawstring (see Figs. 7.10 and 7.11). Made of burlap and printed with the name of the shoe manufacturer, it was salvaged from the wastebasket and heavily embroidered on both sides; the printing was exploited with stitchery on each letter so the words can be read. Because burlap is so loosely woven and is hardly rain repellent, I interlined the bag with plastic (part of a dry cleaner's bag) and then put in a regular lining of burnt orange cotton. The ends of the drawstring were wrapped with threads picking up the colors used in the stitchery. The bag is reasonably practical even if one gets caught in the rain, although I would hesitate to use it in a

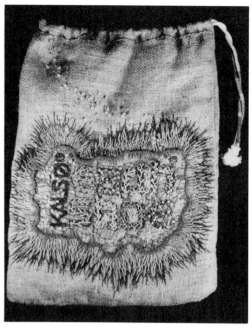

Fig. 7.10 Recycled and stitched shoe bag (author).   **Fig. 7.11** Recycled and stitched shoe bag—view 2.

downpour. It was, of course, sprayed with moisture and dirt repellent when finished.

Do try making bags of many types from the elegant to the casual; it's a good way to use up small amounts of cloth and yarn. Save your old beads, buttons, bells, and baubles for possible use on your bags. Give them the stamp of your personality.

JEWELRY AND BODY ORNAMENTS

Bracelets, neckpieces—the larger, more dramatic version of the necklace—earrings, pendants, brooches—all these have been interpreted in fiber with stunning results in many instances. We see, of course, the familiar and commonplace necklaces and other jewelry, usually macraméd, sold by the armload at craft fairs. Many of these are attractive enough in a very ordinary way. But fiber jewelry seen in galleries and exhibitions is far beyond that ground out for mass sale. The work designed by serious fiber artists is daring in concept, execution and in materials used. One sees fur, feathers, junk, clay, strange and exotic beads—themselves sometimes large enough to stand alone as minisculptures—hair, twine, rope, metal, shells,

86

mica, leather—all these and more are combined with fiber to create works which dazzle the onlooker.

One need not be a fiber virtuoso to be able to make some very lovely jewelry pieces, satisfying to create, wear, and give away, even to sell! When beginning a jewelry project, decide generally what you want to convey in the piece. Is it elegance, whimsy; is it funky, casual, stark, exuberant, small, large? Some kind of rough sketch(es) can be helpful, although once the work is under way new thoughts will probably occur to you which will amend the initial idea. Let your fancy roam where it will, to get the utmost satisfaction from working up the piece. Bypaths and side roads are often much more interesting than the main highway.

Once the general direction has been formulated decide which procedure would be best to implement the concept. Gather the materials together with a view toward appropriateness in color, texture, and harmony.

Consider a necklace which is asymetrical rather than the usual symetrical design. Consider, too, a departure from the usual methods of crochet or macramé when designing the necklace (or pendant, brooch, bracelet, etc.). A stuffed appliquéd medallion might be nifty on a chain; a patchwork neck-piece, lightly quilted, could double as a chest warmer in winter. You could try making a wide-cuff bracelet of wire needle-lace (perhaps caging in bits of beach glass, beads, shells, stones, etc.) in two or three colors of wire—silver, gold, copper. Don't settle for the obvious solutions but stretch the imagination toward the as yet untried.

Body ornaments—as opposed to body coverings, which are really garments—decorate the body with somewhat more substance than jewelry. Biblike constructions tying in the back, wide collars, capelets, arm bands, knotted overgarments, body fringes, even neckpieces with fringes going to the floor (!), breast plates, and any number of decorative adjuncts to one's primary garments are within the realm of body ornaments. Perhaps the recognition given to body ornaments by many of today's artists/craftspeople is a repudiation of the Victorian distaste—at least on the surface!—for the human body. (Most of us have heard of the draped piano legs chastely referred to as "limbs" in Victorian living rooms.) Whatever has generated the current interest in body ornaments, the products resulting from that interest are certainly imaginative and celebrate a joy in the human body with its marvelous complexities.

A very simple body ornament is an over-the-head dress-length accessory (see Fig. 7.12) consisting of two narrow rectangles attached at each shoulder with waist-buttoned tabs on each side to keep the rectangles in place as they hang down front and back. The ornament can be just that with rather narrow rectangles (about the width of a muffler), or it can be transformed into more of a garment, the two pieces meeting at each side where the buttoned tabs hold them together. Resembling a tabard and medieval in feeling, this ornament is a perfect foil for any design interpretation which occurs to its maker. It can have all-over stitchery, abstract appliqué, or quilting; it can be crocheted, or knotted. Fabrics used can range from elegant silk, satin, velvet, or unwaled corduroy to down-to-earth denim,

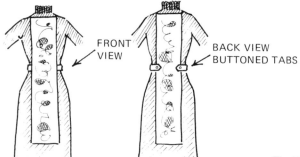

FRONT VIEW

BACK VIEW
BUTTONED TABS

Fig. 7.12 Over-the-head dress-length accessory.

unbleached muslin, or some of the lovely Indian fabrics. It can be trimmed with mirrors, beads, lace, braid, fringe, tassels, macramé—anything you can dream up. Try one; it (with you in it) could be sensational!

A necklet can be a simple or ornate band with fringes falling anywhere from a few inches to floor length. Worn over a simple body suit with pants or skirt it could look very dramatic. The neckband itself can be stitched, quilted, appliquéd, or crocheted or any of the fiber procedures which seem appropriate to the feeling of the piece can be used.

Try a set of armlets: cuffs, several inches wide fitting over a good portion of the forearm. Lavishly embellished with stitchery, imaginatively crocheted, knotted, or knitted, they can be colorful accessories worn on the bare arm or over a long-sleeved turtleneck. If you make the armlets of something non-stretchy (as opposed to crocheting or knitting) you must include buttons and buttonholes or loops so they can be easily put on and taken off. Try to think of fastenings which enhance the armlets and which are themselves a design element.

You will undoubtedly think of many other kinds of wild and wonderful body ornaments. Give your fantasies full range when designing any body ornament. They are, after all, an extension of the individual personality and can be whimsical, funny, flamboyant, stark, or dramatic. Let yourself go!

Fig. 7.13 Example of Indian sequin embroidery on satin collar (collection of the author).

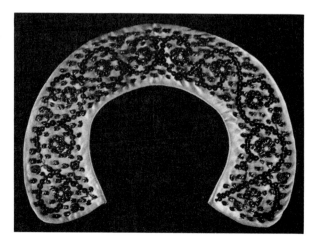

Clothing can reflect the interests and individuality of the fiber artist. Scarves, hats, mittens, leg and shoulder warmers, vests, as well as sweaters, skirts, dresses, pants, and shirts can all, in the hands of the fiber artists, be lifted in appearance from the mundane to the one-of-a-kind and become, whether humorous or beautiful, a joy to make, wear, and look at.

We see (and I notice this particularly in Cambridge where I teach) evidence all around of the use of the personal touch on clothing. The addition of lace to blue jeans, stitchery, patchwork, and applique on shirts, pants, skirts, jackets, and dresses; designs of buttons and beads being used on all kinds of garments. One thinks of the famous "Pearlies" of London with their intricate button designs on their clothing. I read recently in the October 1975 issue of *Crafts*, the publication of the Crafts Advisory Committee, London, England, that the Pearlies are worried about the growing shortage of pearl buttons and the possible effect this will have on their button trimming. They are appealing to anyone who has spare buttons to send them to the Pearly King of Lambeth, 61 Surr St., London N1.

In an age where the individual is being submerged in technocracy and impersonal and shoddy workmanship, the additions one makes to one's garments are a reaffirmation of one's selfhood. Join the movement; make the clothes you wear be truly your own. Many times a tired garment can be revived by using it as a base upon which to work some contemporary designing.

Fig. 7.14 Patchwork and stitchery on T-shirt (author).

A good place to start is with denim shirts, especially those which are well washed but not so worn that the fabric is easily rent apart. Decide what fiber method is personally attractive and express yourself with abandon. The chances are that the final result, whether stitched, patched, appliquéd, fringed, encrusted with crocheted motifs, or whatever, will lift the tired shirt out of the doldrums into new life and service.

One project I enjoyed was doing some rather elegant-in-feeling appliqué on a soft 100 percent wool muffler. I used velvet and silks in an abstract appliqué design on each end of the muffler so the ends as they hung down were equally eye-catching. Stitchery was used with the appliqué and small randomly placed gold seed beads were sewn on. The underside of the muffler ends were lined to cover the wrong side of the work. The lining also served to weight the ends so they hung nicely. The work was sprayed with moisture and dirt repellant when finished to ensure its standing up to the elements. This is an easy, quickly worked project yielding interesting results without the hours and hours of time required in the creation of some of the more ambitious undertakings.

Other smaller items of wearing apparel which lend themselves to dramatization are ties, gloves, knee socks, and hats. Some of the hats resulting from the fertile imagination and daring execution of fiber artists are valid as wall hangings when not in use. Shirley Fink, an extremely talented weaver and teacher whom I've mentioned previously, makes "purse hangings, hat hangings, hanging hangings"—as quoted from her business announcement which is called *Wear 'em or Hang 'em.*

Ms. Fink's creations are woven delights with unexpected pockets, dangling elements, unusual types of yarns mixed together, and offbeat color combinations. Crocheting, quilting, knitting, and stitchery can be used to design hats with flair and distinction. One of the quickest ways to develop a hat is by crochet. Any basic hat pattern will do to form the hat shape or you can make up your own. A hat is, after all, a bowl-shaped form, which can be fitted to one's head to be sure if the foundation shape is wearable. This simple shape is achieved by crocheting a circle, about 3 inches in diameter, and increasing stitches in successive rows round and round until, when trying it on, it goes on the head. Then start decreasing to form the bowl shape. From then on, how one works up the balance of the hat is subject to the ingenuity and originality of the maker.

Consider all kinds of novelty yarns and unusual colors; try working a crocheted relief design on the outer surface of the hat, perhaps with long crocheted ends tipped with bobbles, beads, pieces of fur, bells, or any other interesting oddments. If you want a brim to the hat, consider a convoluted ruffle or perhaps a quilted brim, made separately and then sewn on to the crocheted bowl shape. Stitchery might meander all over your hat to accent it with an additional element. Here again, let your fancy wander and release any residue of inhibitions still remaining in regard to fiber interpretation. One thing you can be certain of: your hat will express your personality and will not be an anonymous item ground out by the hundreds in some factory! Garments made as experimental projects, whether they be small things like ties or large design expressions such as voluminous cloaks or clerical vestments, are witness to the cry for continued recognition of personhood in an impersonal society. We *will not* totally knuckle under to the world of the computer!

CONTAINERS

Many people are charmed by containers—baskets, boxes, vaselike cylinders, and planters. The explosion of myriad types of planters in almost every art/craft show, sale, and fair is an indication not only of the popularity of plants themselves, but of a sensitivity to the kind of container in which they are grown. Although wood, metal, plastic, and ceramic are the most typical materials used in making planters, fiber plant holders lined with protective plastic or glass are also practical. The softness of fiber is very compatible with the growing plants, especially when lovely muted, earth-colored fibers are used. The planters can be worked up in crochet, macramé, coiling, or any fiber technique amenable to turning out a pot-shaped form. It is well to remember that the plant holder is a setting for a growing plant, and the holder should not compete with the plant itself for attention. Otherwise the plant and the container will vie for attention, a detrimental situation for both. This does not mean that a planter must be pedestrian in design and dull in execution. It can and should be as original and handsome as one can devise, not flamboyant but rather a low-keyed lovely complement to the living growth it contains.

The uses we all find for boxes are almost endless. As people are charmed by planters, so are many of us entranced by beautiful boxes, with their function as containers almost secondary to their intrinsic attraction as objects apart from use. In addition to boxes made of wood, metal, ceramic, stone, ivory, and many other much more exotic materials, we are seeing fiber boxes which may be woven, knotted, coiled, crocheted, quilted, and many times enhanced by top stitchery on the surface of the box form.

If one desires to make a box, stabilization of the form must be considered, with technical steps taken to ensure firmness of the form. Depending on procedure used, stabilization can be achieved in several ways. If one wishes to make a quilted box an interior cardboard stiffening can be used to hold the shape. An existing box can be covered with quilted sections seamed to fit the box, or the cardboard can be cut to fit the pieces of quilting, with the quilting seamed and the cardboard lining fitted inside the quilted box form. If this is done, one should consider that the inside of the box would not be very attractive if left with the cardboard showing. To overcome this problem, one can glue an attractive decorative paper to the cardboard before slipping it into the quilted shell; then after fitting both quilted shell and paper-covered cardboard together the top edge of both, the cardboard lining and quilted cover should be glued together so the two are now one unit with no shifting or slipping.

Another way to get around the exposed cardboard lining problem is to

Fig. 7.15 Coiled container (author).

Fig. 7.16 Detail of coiled container.

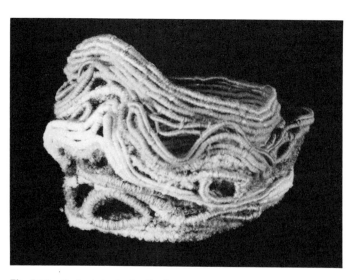

Fig. 7.17 Coiled planter (author).

cover the cardboard with fabric, cutting the fabric large enough to turn over at least ½ inch on the side which will face the raw side of the quilting and glue firmly, allowing about ⅛ inch of cloth to above the cardboard. Then fit the two units together and sew the top edge of the quilting to the top edge of the fabric that projects above the cardboard, melding the two into one non-shifting entity.

Top stitchery can, of course, augment the quilting if desired.

A simple padded box shape with surface stitchery can be made, and its form strengthened in just the same manner as is used in constructing a quilted box, inserting the padding between the cardboard and outer shell.

If a box shape is made with sturdy cord, heavy strong weaving yarn, twine, or similar firm material using crocheting, coiling or knotting, the box will need no extra stabilization because these materials are very stiff when worked.

Crocheted, coiled, or knotted cylinders and vaselike forms may be very effective in their own right. However, dried grasses and other plant materials seem especially suited to this kind of "weed holder."

Basket forms, whether deep bowls, abstract shapes generally concave in nature, shallow traylike objects with just a hint of sides, or utilitarian straightforward baskets, are all forms with which one can experiment with little difficulty once the procedures of crochet, knotting, coiling, etc., are familiar. These things work up quite quickly—unless you work on a grand scale!—with correspondingly quick results. This is encouraging, especially when one is just beginning. If one begins with a rather small project and sees it completed in a relatively short length of time, it is likely to be a spur toward tackling larger, more ambitious works.

QUILTS

No section on functional things to make would be complete without a brief mention of quilts. Quilts have been resurrected from attics, are being snapped up at upcountry auctions and flea markets, and dug up out of old trunks and cedar chests. Quilts are part of American folk art with new respect and recognition being given to the artists of yesterday who turned out so many masterpieces. Consequently, contemporary artists are lending their talents toward creating updated versions of the quilt with startling, sometimes amusing, and frequently stunning results.

An exhibition mounted at De Cordova Museum in Lincoln, Massachusetts, during the summer of 1975, entitled "Bed and Board," featured contemporary and Shaker furniture, and quilts, both traditional and avant garde in concept. The quilts were hung on the museum walls so one could study closely the full designs and workmanship. The traditional types were mostly geometric designs meticulously worked, often machine stitched. The contemporary types were wildly varied in theme, execution shape, and materials chosen. Some were mildly risqué, a few macabre,

Fig. 7.18 Quilted banner used as porch door sign (Betsy Cannon).

others satirical, with a few whimsical, almost surrealistic in feeling. Then there were those with strong abstract designs reminiscent of paintings. The artists, both men and women, exploited to extreme lengths the possibilities of the quilt as an art form which made this show provocatively exciting.

The procedure for quilting (discussed in Chapter 3, section on quilting) is simple. The idea you convey, if you decide to make a quilt, is what will made your quilt either a simply competent exercise or a vibrant and original personal statement. The quilt may incorporate unusual features. For example: a child's quilt can have elements on its surface which can be buttoned or snapped (even zippered) on and off to make the quilt a plaything as well as a warming coverlet. A quilted landscape with removable trees, buildings, and vehicles that can be reassembled in different locations on the fabric landscape might be a quiet pastime for a child confined to bed. A vegetable-motif quilt with removable cloth—perhaps stuffed—vegetables and a quilted salad bowl at one end might be fun for a small youngster to learn about vegetables as well as to mix a "salad" in the bowl. Pockets with stuffed animals in them and flower blossoms which can be buttoned and unbuttoned in their centers are other ideas. I am certain many other novel approaches to the child's quilt will occur once thought is directed to the project. Similarly, if your quilt is an adult-oriented project, ideas will flow once the decision is made to make a quilt.

STRAPS AND BANDS

How many uses do we have for bands and straps in our daily living? Guitar straps, belts, head-bands, watch straps, bag straps, book straps, camera straps—there are many more I'm sure I haven't thought of. Any of these bands and straps can be a personal statement even though the item is a relatively background prop. Woven, knotted, braided, stitched, or crocheted bands are colorful, sturdy, and functional. When making a strap strength, of course, is one of the prime considerations and one which will be a factor in the material chosen for the strap. A strap might have to be interlined in addition to being lined for extra body. Whatever method used for straps, they can be fun to make and can be the basis of a gratifying personal statement.

Fiber art is a lovely way to use one's hands, and is an excellent medium for the creation of functional and nonfunctional design statements. It is desirable to enlarge one's experimental horizons to encompass both these avenues of creativity.

8 Design Exercises

For those who wish to experiment with fiber techniques already familiar to them design exercises are very helpful. As one studies the various aspects of design, different avenues of approach come to mind which give one a fresh slant on one's work. Many artist/craftspeople, already creating satisfactory and successful pieces, are searching for innovative ways to present their fiber ideas. New directions explored will tax ingenuity and imagination into more demanding expression of these ideas.

Problem-solving—deliberately setting oneself a problem and working out its solution—is a good way to help engender design awareness. Stronger, more sensitive work is likely to result from this sort of struggle. There are many design exercises one can do to aid in self-development. Sharper powers of observation, more introspective analyses of design situations, broader knowledge of materials and their possibilities, and heightened appreciation of color use—these are the harvest one reaps from design study and exercises.

Inevitably, in trying unfamiliar ways of design presentation there will be failures. Sometimes discouragement is so acute that consideration is given to abandoning exploration of new directions and to remain where success is more assured. It is not uncommon among all of us to enjoy and desire praise and appreciation for our accomplishments. However, it is well to remember that when engaging in the arts the motivation is generally self-fulfillment. If a work satisfies its creator, that should be sufficient. If others, too, like it that is a bonus. "Success is a result, not a goal," a statement attributed to Gustave Flaubert, is a good reminder for all of us. Do your best and stretch your capabilities in whatever direction exploration and experimentation lead. Learning almost inevitably accompanies the effort.

The exercises described in this chapter are only a few among the many design problems one can undertake. Undoubtedly as you read about these exercises other possibilities will come to mind. Jot your ideas down in your notebook (if you keep one—and I hope you do!) for further study. Many results of exercises are catalysts for developing finished works. Some of the problems seem very simple, but in the actual carrying out of the exercise the apparent simplicity is often found to be deceptive. Save your solutions for future reference, or at least make notes regarding those solutions. It is surprising how useful these records can be when or if a confrontation with a similar design problem occurs in the future.

Fig. 8.1 *Untitled*—stitchery using limited number of different stitches (Martha Liller).

Fig. 8.2 Detail of *Untitled*.

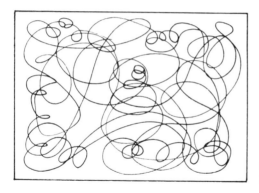

Fig. 8.3 Fill in selected areas to develop a cohesive design.

EXERCISE #1

Provide yourself with a sheet of white paper at least 8½ ″ × 11 ″ or larger and a felt pen in black or a dark color. Close your eyes, feel with your fingers for the paper's edges, then move the pen freely and relaxedly over the paper in a flowing manner without lifting the pen or stopping the movement. Engage the whole arm with a loose, tension-free motion rather than the wrist only. Don't be disturbed if you run off the paper's edges but try to confine yourself within the paper space. When you sense that the paper is filled with pen lines, open your eyes and analyze the linear pattern you have drawn. Choose three or four colors in pastels, Cray-Pas, felt pens, or watercolors and select sections of the pattern to fill with color to develop a unified design from the mass of lines. Many times the abstract design lifted thus is effective enough to warrant being worked up in fabric using stitchery or other procedures which would interpret it most effectively.

This exercise is a good tension reliever and helps overcome the tightness which sometimes occurs when one tries very hard to design in the abstract. Often a concentrated and earnest effort results in work which reflects anxiety or a cramped attitude. However, with closed eyes, a loose arm movement, and pen flowing uninterruptedly over the paper, anxieties dissipate and surprisingly graceful, rhythmic, linear patterns emerge. The problem-solving aspect comes, of course, when choices must be made among the maze of lines and spaces to achieve a cohesive entity. (See Fig. 8.3 and try filling in a selected area to develop a satisfactory design.)

EXERCISE #2

Continuing the study of linear problems (and this time with eyes open!) develop a pleasing design on a piece of fabric using couched down yarns as lines. Confine the stitchery to couching only, depending on the rhythm and flow of the couched lines for design interest. Although several types of yarns may be combined, both thick and thin, it is more difficult to develop an

Fig. 8.4 Weathered railroad tie. Note interesting
linear pattern of weather-beaten wood.

Fig. 8.5 Another railroad tie with linear interest.

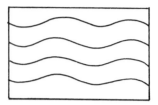

Fig. 8.6 Monotonous spatial relationship.

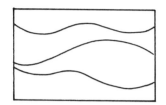

Fig. 8.7 Irregular spatial relationship is more aesthetically pleasing.

interesting design with one kind of yarn only, and consequently, it is more of a challenge if you limit yourself in this way. Naturally, spatial relationships assume great importance in designing—especially so in this exercise because of the limitations imposed by method and material. If the couched lines are arranged evenly, monotony will result (see Fig. 8.6). Check the design for placement so the solution to the problem will be pleasing to the eye. Contrast Figure 8.6 with Figure 8.7. If you like your solution sufficiently to make it up as a finished project, so much the better.

EXERCISE #3

Select a group of fruits or vegetables (or both) and slice them across and lengthwise. One usually thinks of obvious fruits such as apples and oranges, but try ones less often used such as pomegranates, bananas, and some of the tropical fruits seen frequently in supermarkets. Cabbage cores, red cabbage slices, peppers, mushrooms, peas in a pod, celery cross sections—all these and many more provide lovely design inspiration when studied closely. Make a series of pen or pencil drawings of these cross or lengthwise sections beginning with a representational rendering, then a stylized drawing, finally an abstract drawing, which uses only those elements of the object which you wish to stress. (See Figs. 8.8, 8.9, and 8.10.) Try to visualize these objects as forms, disassociated from what they are. Look closely at the patterns of the sections and try to see how they would translate into designs. Even if you are convinced that you can't draw, try the exercise, doing the best you can. When you have finished with your drawings and observations, make a lovely salad of your sections and enjoy a healthy and visually beautiful lunch!

In doing an exercise of this kind, line, shape, and pattern are the specific areas of interest. However, take careful note of color variations and combinations also. Many people get into a color rut, rarely deviating from a set of "favorite" colors. It would be helpful to try to overcome color prejudices and have an open mind toward all hues and their possible roles in one's work.

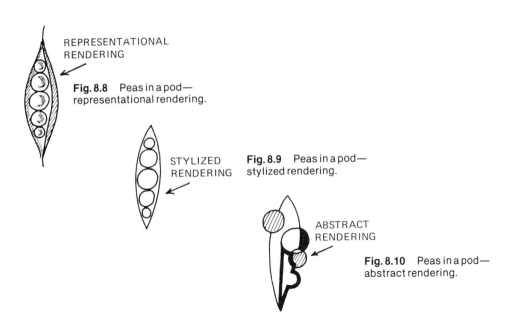

REPRESENTATIONAL RENDERING

Fig. 8.8 Peas in a pod—representational rendering.

STYLIZED RENDERING

Fig. 8.9 Peas in a pod—stylized rendering.

ABSTRACT RENDERING

Fig. 8.10 Peas in a pod—abstract rendering.

EXERCISE #4

The comments above regarding color lead into the next problem to consider. Choose the two colors most distasteful to you and work with them to develop a design. This may be done on paper or with fabric and can be worked out two- or three-dimensionally. Considering all the design principles (balance, proportion, harmony, unity, contrast, emphasis, rhythm), try to rise above the antipathy you feel toward the colors you are working with and concentrate on creating an entity which satisfies all the requirements of a good design. Probably the simplest way to do this problem is with paper in the two chosen colors, cutting and gluing down shapes on a third sheet of paper which serves only as a foundation and which should be completely covered so as not to introduce a third color. Or the foundation sheet itself can be one of your two colors. As one works with color, even those personally unappealing, dislikes often fade and a more flexible, sophisticated attitude regarding color is adopted, thus broadening one's design options.

EXERCISE #5

Achieving balance and harmony in spatial relationships often presents problems for the beginning designer. A good fiber idea executed with careful workmanship often falls short in the placement of the various elements of the composition, thus weakening the whole design. Insufficient attention is paid to arrangement and the effect it has on both positive and negative spaces, resulting in a monotonous presentation. Often just a little

101

readjustment will transform a dull piece into a dynamic statement. There are many basic design books to which one can refer (see the Bibliography) for guidance on this point and it is well worthwhile to take the time for study. One cannot rely alone on technique to create a valid work. Proficiency in method is the means with which a concept is expressed; but the idea, and how it is presented in the design, is the essence.

A deceptively simple problem in placement involves working with dots, all the same size, arranging them on a sheet of paper in a unified design with focus and balance. Black press-adhesive dots (available at most stationers) on white paper or vice versa are recommended to work out this exercise. Using shapes—in this instance, dots—identical in size with one another is much more difficult than working with those of different sizes. You may find that achieving a spatially interesting result is a more demanding challenge than one would expect. As mentioned before, save your solutions for future reference material.

EXERCISE #6

Still concentrating on spatial relationships, work out a good abstract composition using cloth shapes appliquéd on a background fabric. The shapes can be of several colors, printed or plain cloth, but simplicity should be stressed. Avoid a busy, cluttered look with a lot of small elements which are unessential to the overall design. This exercise can be worked out on paper also but cloth is so tactilely pleasing that many people prefer using it. Study the finished design and check the placement of the component parts in relation to one another. Before the shapes are sewn down be sure the spaces, negative and positive, are handled well. Avoid just touching the edge of one piece with another, i.e., "kissing" the edge. The design will look better if you leave some space between elements or overlap them. Working out abstract compositions is a good way to become aware of and see shapes simply as shapes. Many times we get involved with what a shape represents. Vision gets clouded by the representation and we don't really *see* the shape—only a tree which may look lopsided, for example, and we get disturbed. Forget, for the time being, representation and really concentrate on shape only.

EXERCISE #7

A good way to experiment both with shapes and with color is to work out a composition with art tissue overlays. Do this on a large sheet of white drawing paper using a package of assorted color art tissue (available at art supply stores). Choose a group of colors—not more than four—and tear or cut shapes out of the tissue, arranging them on the white paper, overlapping the shapes in some areas to get color variations. You need not confine yourself to the paper's edge; some of the shapes can extend beyond the edge if it would improve the composition. Note not only placement of your tissue pieces, but the subtle color changes which occur when two or more pieces overlap one another. When the arrangement suits you, glue it down with small dabs of Elmer's glue which dries clearly. Beautiful designs for future development can come from this exercise. One of my students worked her exercise result into a fabric hanging; it was most interesting to see the paper beginning and the fabric ending side by side.

EXERCISE #8

Reverse appliqué, one of the more intricate types of appliqué, provides the basis for the next exercise. For this problem, I would suggest using origami paper, the colors of which are brilliant and cheerful to use. Origami paper is readily available in art supply stores and is inexpensive. Choose three or four colors of the paper and stack them on top of one another. What you are going to do is to develop a design by cutting into the paper, layer by layer, revealing the next color underneath. This exercise is a good preparation for trying reverse appliqué in cloth. It's much less expensive in time and money to work out miscalculations with paper than with fabric. It is a good idea when solving this problem to think out a general plan before making the first cut. Each cut is final, so proceed slowly and consider the successive steps before taking them. Here again, as in several other exercises, the finished solution may look lovely translated in cloth. Observe the colors, as well as the shapes, in relation to each other. When all the cuts have been made and the design completed, glue the edges of the papers to one another with dots of white glue to hold the whole thing together. Try this problem in several sets of colors and different compositions. Doing this problem will give you heightened respect for the artistry of the Cuna Indians and their beautiful reverse appliquéd work.

EXERCISE #9

One of the attributes of fiber art which pleases the senses is texture. Textures with their varied qualities invite the observer not only to look but to touch (even though the invitation often should not be accepted, due to exhibition regulations!). When we look about us in the natural world, thousands of different textures beckon and charm us with their infinite variety. How sad it is when many people do not notice this richess of aspect, available to all. A good way to sensitize oneself to texture is by close observation with both the naked eye and the magnifying glass—the microscope, too, if one is available for use. In this exercise observation and drawing of texture is the area of interest. Gather together a group of natural objects such as a piece of bark, rocks, shells, nuts, seed pods, pine cones, sea urchins, starfish, moss, lichens, and the like. Look at these things carefully, first with just your "bare" eye as my small son used to say, and then with a magnifying glass.

Fig. 8.11 Tree bark with textural interest.

Observe the structures, striations, roughness, smoothness, patterns, all aspects of the objects. Then make a series of drawings of these textures using pen and ink, felt pen, or pencil. Try to render the textures as you see them, and contrast one with another—the smoothness of one thing as compared to the roughness of another. Giving careful attention to the natural world all around us feeds the imagination, providing fertile ground in which design will germinate. One becomes sensitized to natural beauty which in turn enriches the soul. "Consciousness-raising" is the fashionable term used these days to describe becoming more acutely aware of social problems and conditions. We should also raise our consciousness to our environment. Maybe then we would not so heedlessly endanger it.

EXERCISE #10

Departing momentarily from concern with the natural world, the next problem deals with man-made pattern and its manipulation. For this exercise it is recommended that a piece of striped material, at least ½ yard long be used for the experiment. With the striped material, evolve a cohesive design by manipulation of the patterned material in any way you wish to get an interesting composition. Try folding, pleating, crushing, gathering, puckering—all distortions one can think of to use the stripes for the creation of a balanced, harmonious design. Stripes have a dynamism of their own which can be exploited; the challenge lies in bringing all this energetic visual interest into a focused coherent unit. With the wide exposure of op art, stripes, rectangles, squares, etc., have been assaulting our senses in exciting ways. It is intriguing to try to bring the stripe to heel by adroit manipulation. This kind of exercise can be done with other types of patterned material too, of course, and you may wish to experiment with several different patterns, augmenting the solutions with stitchery for accent and drama.

EXERCISE #11

In Praise of Hands, written by Octavio Paz, is a book that celebrates the handcrafts of artists all over the world. How remarkable are the human hands and how much we take them for granted! The following exercise uses the hand as inspiration for design. Make a series of pen or pencil sketches using your own hand in various positions as the subject. Begin with representational renderings, then go on to stylizing the shapes of the hand you drew in the first sketch. Finally go on to abstract design, putting into the composition only those elements of the stylization you need to make a good design (see Fig. 8.12). The hand is not an easy subject to draw unless you are an excellent draftsperson. You'll probably use lots of paper! While working with your hand as inspiration consider all the intricacies of this marvelous instrument and what positive accomplishments it is capable of achieving. Analyze the drawings and don't worry if the literal renderings are less than ideal. The thought process necessary to make a graphic transition from a realistic to a stylized concept then on to an abstract concept is a good way to enlarge one's way of thinking when design options are being considered. The excellence of the drawings themselves is of lesser importance than the amount of mental effort expended to make them.

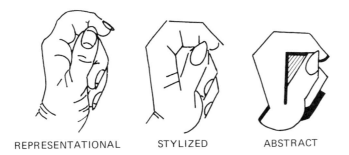

REPRESENTATIONAL   STYLIZED   ABSTRACT

Fig. 8.12   Human hand—representational, stylized, and abstract renderings.

Fig. 8.13 Human face—stylized and abstract renderings.

EXERCISE #12

Our final exercise uses the human face as the subject for design. This time, there will be no transitional series of drawings made, i.e., representational, stylized, abstract. Rather, make numerous small thumbnail sketches both stylized and abstract on a sheet of drawing paper, using elements of the face as the basis for design (see Fig. 8.13).

I am sure your designs will be much better! Think about reducing the components of the face—eyes, nose, mouth—to barest essentials of shape and rearrange those shapes in various cohesive designs. When the sheet is filled study the designs; choose the one most pleasing to you and work it up in a large, careful drawing, perhaps using color this time. Many times these small thumbnail sketches will be reminiscent of primitive fetishes, carvings, paintings, and sculptures—almost atavistic in feeling. Perhaps the gap between primitive culture and our highly civilized (?) technological society is slimmer than we care to think.

In any of these exercises, the possibilities for developing finished works stemming from the problems and their solutions, are many. Use these problems as a means of generating ideas and pursuing new avenues of experimentation.

To extend one's mental range of design possibilities, it is helpful to consider descriptive words relating to the qualities regarding the appearance and the mood of one's works. Make a list of as many descriptive nouns, verbs, and adjectives as you can think of in relation to what constitutes fiber art and the materials from which it is created. It is surprising how many qualities of condition come to mind as a deliberate effort is made to list them. Add to the list as other words come to mind. Keep the list for ready reference when you are stuck in a design quandary. Perhaps one of your words will lead you out of an impasse.

Although information on color use is widely available in instructional books on art, a few comments on color are included here with the hope that they might be helpful. Most of us are familiar with the terms primary, secondary, and complementary colors; *primary* colors are red, yellow, and blue; *secondary* colors (made by mixing two primaries) are orange, green, and violet; *complementary* colors are those colors opposite each other on the color wheel; *tertiary* colors are achieved by the mixture of a secondary color with a primary color, i.e., red with orange gives red-orange; yellow with orange gives orange-yellow; blue with violet gives blue-violet, etc.

Hue is the quality that differentiates one color from another.

Tone is the brightness content of a color.

Chroma is the saturation quality of a color, or the quantity of color content.

Value in relation to color is the consideration of how all these foregoing characteristics of a color are working together and the color's consequent complete visual effect.

Warm and *cool:* we speak of *warm* (reds, yellows) and *cool* (blues, greens) colors.

Tints are made by the addition of white to a color.

Shades are made by the addition of black to a color. Tints and shades are ways of varying hues.

Grays: mixing equal parts of complementary colors results in a richer gray than that obtained by mixing white with black.

Broken color is the term used to describe the placement of small spots of color next to each other, allowing the "mixture" of color to take place in the eye—the technique used by the Impressionist painters. If red and blue are placed next to each other, the eye will mix them and a shimmering irridescent violet will result, with a more intense effect than if it had been mixed directly. One can utilize the broken color technique to mix any colors desired, depending on the eye to do the work.

Monochromatic colors are the variations made using one hue only, depending on tints, tones, and shades for degree of intensity and value.

Triadic colors are any three colors equally distant on the color wheel. Remember that the color wheel consists of red, orange, yellow, green, blue, and violet—the colors of the spectrum.

Related colors are achieved by mixing a color or a neutral (white, gray, and black) with each of the colors used in a color scheme, thus giving each a common ingredient and producing a feeling of unity.

Limited colors are achieved by the selection of a specific number of colors and mixing colors within that group.

Prejudiced colors are those combinations not generally accepted by mass popular taste, i.e., pink and yellow, orange and purple, cerise and orange, and so on. I must confess it is difficult for me to think of any prejudicial color schemes because I've overcome my own color notions to such an extent that no color scheme seems too outlandish!

Color harmony: it is helpful for a designer to accept the notion that all colors are harmonious with one another. One need only to refer to nature to verify this idea. No longer need we be hamstrung by outdated color inhibitions. How and in what proportional formulas the colors are used is the acid test of color mastery.

Vibrating colors occur when complementary colors of equal value are in juxtaposition with each other. They vibrate when viewed. Much of the psychydelic art we've seen in recent years has depended on this color vibration for its visual impact.

Enjoy color and design experimentation. Become aware of various color nuances and explore many design solutions. All of this experience with color and design problems will be most useful in making your fiber pieces more dynamic to view and more satisfying to create.

9 Don't Work in a Vacuum

Feelings of isolation can overtake those who are working in the visual arts. Unlike most performing artists who generally work in concert with their fellows, the visual artist, more commonly working alone, is often prey to the feeling of being a "voice in the wilderness." At times like these it is not uncommon for the visual artist to "go dry"—be devoid of ideas and creative stimulus—unless positive steps are taken to alleviate loneliness of spirit. Some suggestions to help overcome these difficulties are the purpose of this chapter. It is hoped that they will be of some help.

GO to exhibitions, galleries, museums, and those outlets where fine works are displayed and sold. Exposure to the works of other artists is valuable not only for visual enjoyment but also to keep one abreast of new directions, developments, and concepts, as well as to provide stimuli for ideas useful in one's personal work. This is not to imply that one should copy what others have done, but new ideas spin off when one studies the accomplishments of colleagues. All avenues of visual art expression—painting, graphics, photography, architecture, sculpture, and textiles—should be within your sphere of interest. Works of silver and goldsmiths, glassblowers, woodworkers, as well as top-quality commercial artists can spark ideas for further development. A stunning advertising layout can generate inspiration for a design which, when fully realized, can be far removed from commercialism. One thing I've found quite helpful, is to take notes when looking at other people's work. Jot down observations regarding pieces which are especially noteworthy, either positively or negatively. In future discussions and as reference material these notes can be useful memory joggers.

JOIN craft organizations, art associations, and other groups of artist/craftspeople. Although many of us, burdened by busy time schedules, are not as active as we might wish to be in professional associations, even passive membershp is mutually beneficial to both the organization and the member. Dues paying members are the lifeblood of organizations; if you can also contribute time so much the better. Usually the art and craft organizations mount exhibitions of members' work which gives one a chance to show; some shows are open, others are juried, still others invitational. It is excellent experience to present one's work to public view. And as soon as you do you are vulnerable to the slings and arrows of criticism. While ego is sometimes deflated by adverse comments, on the other hand a favorable reaction is sweet indeed. It is well to be prepared for both! In addition to showings, many organizations publish periodic newsletters and magazines which are very helpful to keep continually aware of what is taking place in the art scene—who is doing what and where.

If you attend group meetings, you will find opportunities for productive and supportive discussion with those in the field. It is soon apparent that situations and feelings personally encountered are shared by practically everyone else in the group. This is reassuring.

Other benefits that may be offered by some arts/crafts associations are reduced or complimentary admission to pertinent events and discounts on workshops and books. Sometimes lectures and slide shows are offered.

SHOW your work when suitable opportunities arise. In addition to the exhibitions mounted by arts and crafts associations, other occasions such as fairs, small exhibits in banks, theatres, office buildings, and schools, as well as fund-raising events are showcases for art works. Show your work, too, to other artists for criticism. "Crit sessions" among artists are worthwhile to gain new perspective on one's efforts. After working on a piece with intense concentration and emotional investment it is easy to lose objectivity regarding the work—the old situation of not being able to "see the forest for the trees"! Independent judgment by colleagues is invaluable for an outside assessment of the work. Whether you agree or disagree with the value judgment made is minor—at least other opinions are given for consideration.

In preparing work for an exhibit be sure it is finished nicely with a proper hanging or supportive device if either is required. Don't expect the people running the exhibit to figure out how a piece is to be displayed. It is advisable to indicate clearly how the piece is to be presented, especially if it is an abstract. (I've been guilty of this in the past, "top and bottom" of a piece being so clear in my mind I unreasonably thought it must, therefore, be clear to everyone! It wasn't. On opening day of the exhibit in which the piece was shown, it was hung upside down. My fault.) If a piece is composed of more than one entity or needs draping or arranging or is in any way complicated to install, send along complete instructions and diagrams for displaying.

If your work has a rod for a hanging device, *don't* use a curtain rod. Many juries for exhibits won't accept pieces which are hung by curtain rods; they reason that all aspects of a piece, hanging device included, should relate to one another; use of a curtain rod indicates to them a disrespect on the part of the artist for the integrity of the work. Choose a rod with care, considering appropriateness to the mood and design of the work it is to accompany. Tasteful and sensitive presentation of a work is an integral part of the whole entity. Poor presentation and improper lighting and hanging can destroy the impact of a work. If, for example, a lacy texture is a feature of a hanging, it would probably benefit by being hung a few inches away from the wall, to allow cast shadows to heighten the drama of that hanging. Again, instructions for unusual installation specifications should be furnished with any work submitted for exhibiting.

Don't be discouraged if, when you submit work to a jury to be passed upon before entrance into a show, it is rejected. It is good to realize when a work is not up to jury standards. One's own standards might, as a consequence, become sharpened and one's self-criticism more acute. There are those instances when one has reason to suspect that a jury is not accurate or fair in its judging; it is easy then to feel aggrieved. However, this situation is not common so it is probably less nerve-wracking to give the jury the benefit of the doubt, accept with good grace their verdict, and try again another time.

TALK to others engaged in the textile arts. When like-minded people get together to compare notes, experiences, and show each other what they are working on, idea spinoff generates other ideas which is the theory behind brainstorming. An informal series of get-togethers of "textile people" held at the home of a very inspiring artist/teacher, Mary Ventre, author of *Crochet*, led to new directions for many of us fortunate enough to attend. We stimulated each other; we shared common problems and grievances. And we, for a time at least, solved the problem of artistic isolation.

TAKE classes in fiber techniques and in design. Art is continually evolving, with new slants on old methods springing into life all the time. Different ways of using materials, both old and new, as well as updated versions of familiar processes—these and other aspects of fiber art are being dealt with and are often taught by contemporary artists. It is worthwhile to avail oneself of such opportunities to expand on one's fund of knowledge, even though one might be already working on an advanced level. Learning and discovery never end, which is what makes the art experience exciting. Investigate the classes and workshops being offered in your area and attend as many as you feel you can. A course in basketry, for instance, might provide new directions in fiber constructions; a class in lace-making may lead to added design expression in one's work. The classes not specifically dealing with one's current focus of interest, but which are tangentially related to the textile world, are well worth considering for enrollment.

It has been my experience, also, that the same curriculum taught by different teachers varies sufficiently to make it advantageous to repeat that subject under different instructors.

Concentrated workshops, generally held on a weekend, are very good when a specific area is the focus. If several areas are dealt with they tend to be diffuse and confusing when compacted into that short period of time. The ones I have attended were all-day sessions, Saturday and Sunday, with lunch breaks. A lot of information on one technique only was given to the students to study and then to use in developing a fiber piece. Each person worked very intensively and there was very little conversation! At the end of those workshops, there was generally mutual discussion and informal comment on the work produced by the students. Sometimes a slide show of master works was shown either at the very beginning or at the end of the session. When looking at very accomplished pieces, it was clear to everyone not how far they'd gone, but how far they had to go! These intensive working and study sessions are exhausting but rewarding.

Design classes are very helpful in guiding the competent technician on the road toward producing well-designed art statements.

An excellent design course in which I participated utilized provocative classroom and home assignments to increase design perception among the students. The creation by the students of a new room environment, accomplished by rearranging the existing classroom furniture, was one problem for group participation and cooperation—a sharp contrast to another assignment which consisted of making a series of contact drawings of buildings. (Contact drawing is done by looking only at the subject being drawn, and not at the paper or the hand doing the drawing. You get some really odd results in the beginning, but the quality of the drawings improve as the number of drawings done increases.)

Classes dealing with principles of design sharpen perception and increase sensitivity and awareness which help one to develop good design judgments. Much of what makes good design is felt intuitively but intuition can be helped along by knowledgeable guidance and maintaining an open, flexible mind.

SUBSCRIBE to the better publications in the field of arts/crafts, such as *Crafts Horizons, Crafts,* and *Shuttle, Spindle and Dyepot.* There are others, too, which you may wish to add to your subscription list. The publications which deal with the world of arts/crafts on an advanced level not only are inspirational but are sources of solid information on the developments within the field on an international basis. They are vastly different from the hobbyist magazines which flood the newstands. Some of the publications such as *Crafts Horizons* and *Crafts* carry reviews of noteworthy exhibits here and abroad with excellent photographs of some of the mentioned works accompanying the reviews. Recent books dealing with relevant subjects are also reviewed. Occasionally there are philosophical disagreements on various aspects of art and craft which are aired in print. These are stimulating and can get the adrenaline flowing!

GIVE your work to good causes when asked to do so. Many movements rely on the generosity of those sympathetic to their aims for their continued existence. A good feeling is engendered by having the ability and willingness to contribute the work of one's hands to those endeavors close to the heart. Generosity, of course, has its own rewards, but the exposure of your work to the eyes of others is an additional, although incidental, reward.

GROW within yourself and you'll grow as an artist. Train the eyes to see more and the mind to absorb more. The philosophies examined, the music heard, the beauty seen, the poetry read—all contribute to the whole personality. The empathy felt toward society's victims, the outrage felt at instances of injustice, the love felt toward fellow human beings—these feelings are an important part of the caring person and a caring person is likely to become a better artist with more significant things to say. Consider the power that certain music has to stir the soul and feed the flames of rebellion against oppression. The singing of the "Soldier's Song" by Irishmen was a crime punishable by death at one time in Ireland's troubled history. The bagpipes were, for a time, considered a weapon of war and their use forbidden. Consider, too, the power of Picasso's antiwar statement, *Guernica*. What a refutation to the persuasions of the warmakers! It is not by chance that some of society's severest critics are the artists, the writers, the poets, and the dramatists. It is not by chance that their expressions are often feared and suppressed by government.

READ all you can in your field. Besides subscribing to relevant publications, look to the public library for material helpful in the search for knowledge. If finances permit, try to assemble a reference library of your own. Many of the good books on textiles are now available in (relatively) inexpensive paperback as well as in hard-cover. While the library is an excellent source for varied and extensive research, you will find it very handy to own a few books that you can turn to for ready reference and inspiration. Of course your design notebook, too, can be a good reference source if it has been filled with clippings and other useful material relating to your sphere of interest—another inducement to begin a notebook.

DON'T be discouraged if your work is not understood or appreciated by others. One's direction in fiber art is very personal and the important person to please is yourself. How other people view your work is really irrelevant. You might even consider a negative reaction to one of your pieces in a positive way—the work wasn't ignored—it was *noticed* by someone, even though hostilely. That's a mildly comforting thought (even if it is "cold comfort") but try not to be upset by anyone else's attitudes relating to your work. Unless you are working primarily to sell, your efforts are for self-fulfillment. As satisfaction with personal progress grows so will the self-confidence that helps inure one against the uncomplimentary comments of others. And every so often an encounter will occur with someone who is on your wavelength, someone who understands and may even like what you are trying to express. Savor these moments to neutralize the bad ones.

HELP other budding artists in any way that you can—encouragement, perhaps tactful guidance (if asked for), a sharing of knowledge, practical tips on how to get over stumbling blocks, or anything you can think of which may be of assistance especially to the interested beginner. Many

Fig. 9.1 Stuffed and quilted whimsical wall-piece (Betsy Cannon).

people were and still are helpful and encouraging to me. Perhaps the one person who lent me the most sensitive and highly valued guidance while she lived in my area was Mary Ventre, to whom I owe a large part of the happiness I derive from working in fiber. Because of personal experience with a kind and concerned mentor I am very aware of the importance of this sharing of knowledge. You may find that while giving someone else a hand your personal learning increases as you strive to keep one step ahead of these talented comers! The give and take of mutual discussion between textile people of varying levels of expertise strengthens a feeling of comaraderie and again demolishes the sense of isolation.

It is hoped that these suggestions may be beneficial and will encourage those who are interested in fiber art to seek out and fraternize with others similarly involved.

Come in out of the cold!

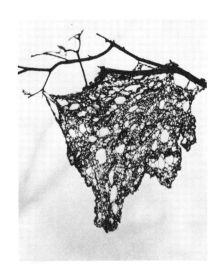

10 Special Techniques –Possibly Unfamiliar

Throughout this book many techniques have been cited as means of expressing ideas in fiber. Although most of the processes mentioned are probably familiar to textile artists, it is possible that some may not be as well known. This chapter will deal with a few of the more uncommon methods.

NEEDLE-LACE

Needle-lace, although ancient in origin, is used by contemporary fiber artists in unconventional and ingenious presentations. Using the detached buttonhole stitch, sometimes called knotless netting, a lovely open unstructured lacy texture can be developed by varying the spatial relationships, thread thicknesses and needle sizes. The tools needed for this type of lace-making are a working board, at least 24 inches square, T-pins, needles, and threads (or yarns). For a working board upon which to make a piece of lace with a minimum of frustration, use a piece of corrugated cardboard, sheet cork, composition board (such as Homesote, available at lumber yards), or anything similar into which you can stick T-pins, pinning the lace down as it is being made. This will allow the lace-maker to see and control the shape of the lace as it enlarges under the fingers.

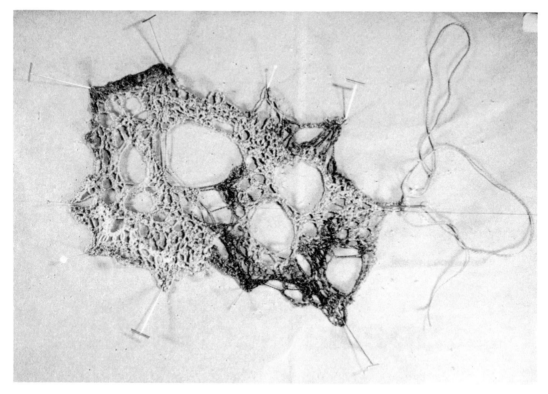

Fig. 10.1 Needle-lace in preliminary stage (author).

To start a piece of lace cut a thread about 6 inches long, knot it at each end, and with a T-pin through each knot, fasten the thread horizontally near the top of the working board (see Fig. 10.2). This will serve as a holding cord as you begin to work the stitches. Then thread a needle with whatever thread you choose to work into lace. Select a needle to accommodate the thread, bearing in mind that a large needle, such as a yarn needle, used with thin thread will give a more open appearance to the texture. Perle cotton, crochet thread, carpet thread, and fine yarn are all good choices for achieving a

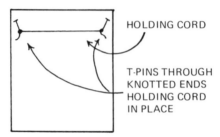

HOLDING CORD

T-PINS THROUGH
KNOTTED ENDS
HOLDING CORD
IN PLACE

Fig. 10.2 Needle-lace—beginning step.

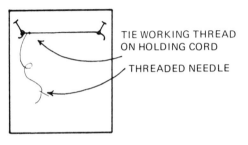

TIE WORKING THREAD
ON HOLDING CORD

THREADED NEEDLE

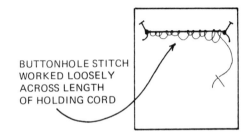

BUTTONHOLE STITCH
WORKED LOOSELY
ACROSS LENGTH
OF HOLDING CORD

Fig. 10.3 Needle-lace—attaching thread.

Fig. 10.4 Needle-lace—buttonhole stitch.

delicate-appearing lace. Tie the working thread which has been threaded into the needle onto the holding cord which has been pinned into place as indicated (see Fig. 10.3). Work the buttonhole stitch *loosely* across the length of the cord (Fig. 10.4), then back and forth again, varying the size of the openings to avoid a monotonous appearance. Work isolated sections of the growing lace, building additional size in small areas then go on to other portions, thus creating an interestingly irregular shape. The looser the stitch, the more open and lacy the texture will appear. Don't use threads much more than 12-14 inches in length to avoid the snarling and knotting which happens sometimes when working with very long threads. When the thread runs out just draw the stitch up very tightly twice and clip off the end. Rethread and resume where you left off. In a piece of completed lace the places where you ended and began again blend in and are all but invisible. Pin

Fig. 10.5 Needle-lace in finishing stage (author).

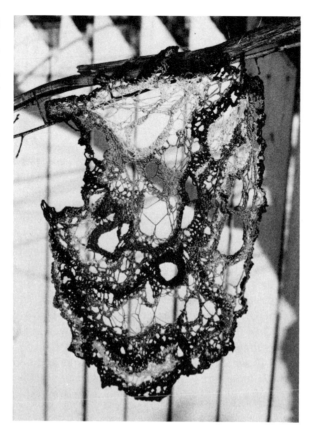

Fig. 10.6 Needle-lace mounted on tree branch (author).

sections just worked in place to control the shape and shift the pins as you proceed. Very shortly your board will bristle with pins, leaving only the immediate working spot free of them. Thread colors and needle sizes can be interchanged at will as can type and thicknesses of threads. Avoid nubbly yarns, though; they are hard to work with in this technique. The fuzzy threads, too, are not as effective as those which work up crisply with a well-defined outline. The gauzy appearance of fuzzy threads obscures the lace work. The ultimate look of the finished lace is always within the control of its maker, who determines the tension variations of the stitches as they are worked. Contrasting very closely stitched areas with very open sections will result in a more interesting texture because of the spatial variables.

The process used for making this free, lacy texture is very simple, but as in many other simple processes, it is very adaptable to individual interpretation. The lace can be left pinned to the working board to be worked on when time permits. If done with threads rather than yarns this kind of lace works up rather slowly; with patience and imagination, however, the end results can be very beautiful.

Pieces of needle-lace can be successfully combined with other textile procedures in one finished piece, or the lace itself can be presented as the sole design element. Pieces of the lace look effective appliquéd to a cloth background on which other textile techniques can be commingled in whatever way is best suited to the overall design. Found objects can be caged underneath the lace; choose a sufficiently tightly worked area to cover them to prevent their slipping out. Shisha mirrors, shells, marbles, beads, buttons, and stones are all possibilities to consider using in conjunction with appliquéd needle-lace. Once you have made up some lace pieces probably many more innovative ideas on what to do with them will occur to you. The same method can be used with much heavier cords, twines, even rope and wire if you wish a robust texture. Then, using the same stitch, manipulate the cords, rope, etc., with your fingers, eliminating use of a needle.

After making a couple of pieces of lace, you will very likely find that you won't need the 6-inch holding cord on which to begin the lace. It can be started by pinning a small loop in place and working around the loop to get the lace underway. However, when one is just beginning to learn how to make this unstructured kind of lace it is easier to have something a little larger to work from, such as a holding cord, rather than a small loop.

One of the lace pieces I made some time ago was done in three shades of a neutral soft brown perle cotton, in an irregular shape with long, very uneven edges. When finished, it was attached at one end to a twiggy branch, the jagged edges hanging down (see Fig. 10.7). It gave the effect of being an ex-

Fig. 10.7 *Extension*—needle-lace attached to twiggy branch (author).

tension of nature because of the harmony of the colors used blending very closely with the coloration of the branch.

Other lace pieces have incorporated rusted metal fragments within the lacy structure; still others have been used in combination with stitchery, quilting, appliqué, and crochet in single entities. There are so many possibilities for a variety of uses in needle-lace—as well as much variation in the thread, yarn, rope, or wire that one can use for its construction—which make it a worthy technique for experimentation.

NEEDLE-WEAVING

A rich, lush texture can be built up by the use of needle-weaving on a cloth backing. Again, as in needle-lace, the process is not difficult, but the effect can be very handsome, especially if color is used sensitively along with a variety of threads.

The needle-weaving is done on long threads laid in straight stitches on a background, those stitches serving as the warp for the weaving (see Fig. 10.8). A simple tabby weave can be used for the weaving or a more compli-

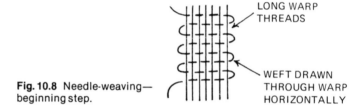

Fig. 10.8 Needle-weaving—
beginning step.

LONG WARP
THREADS

WEFT DRAWN
THROUGH WARP
HORIZONTALLY

cated weaving pattern can be done if desired. Tabby, the weave used in making tapestries, is simply drawing yarn or thread over and under successive threads of the warp, repeating until the end of the row and then returning in the next row reversing the weave done in the previous row. Weaving back and forth in succeeding rows gradually builds a solid woven area (see Fig. 10.9). The straight stitches of the warp can be randomly laid as well as put down in straight rows. The weaving in a random-laid warp is begun at the center junction of the stitches and proceeds from the central core outward (see Figure 10.10). Several threads of the warp, gathered together

SOLID
WOVEN
AREA

Fig. 10.9 Needle-weaving—building
a solid woven area.

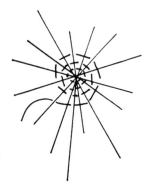

Fig. 10.10 Needle-weaving on randomly laid warp—uneven number of warp threads must be laid down for this type of warp to enable tabby weave to work out mathematically—weave from center outward.

and used as a single unit, can be worked with a buttonhole stitch along their entire length. This can also be done on a single-warp thread. The button-holed warp will gently twist which is a nice variation when a surface is being built. Thickly criss-crossing needle-woven and buttonholed warps is a very effective way in which a surface rich in depth, texture, and color can evolve (see Fig. 10.11). Use of closely related colors rather than widely divergent hues gives a more subtle appearance to the work. The colors, as they appear,

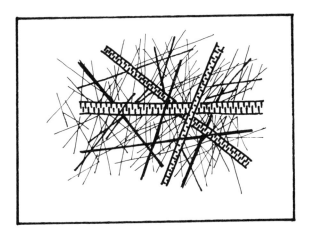

Fig. 10.11 Criss-crossed te::ture of needle-woven and buttonholed warp threads.

disappear, and reappear in the heavily criss-crossed area, interact nicely with one another. It's a fascinating technique to experiment with to get unusual effects for possible use in subsequent projects. A kitchen fork is very handy for controlling distance between the woven rows. Use it to push the rows tightly against each each if a very dense look is desired or to separate the rows if a more open look with exposed warp threads is preferred. If the work is done with a fine-threaded warp this manipulation of the woven rows can be done with the needle. When beginning the weaving, knot the thread and bring it from underneath (wrong side) to the working side where the

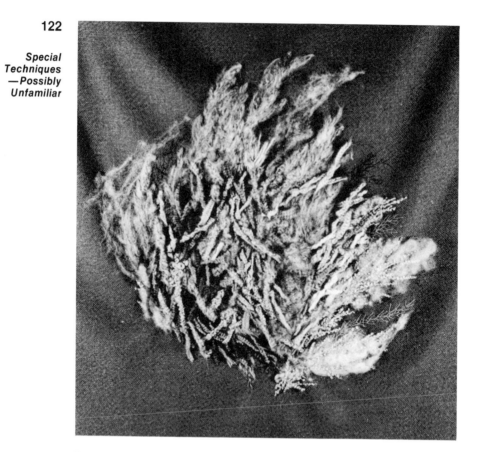

Fig. 10.12 *Emerging Spring*—needle-weaving and stitchery (author).

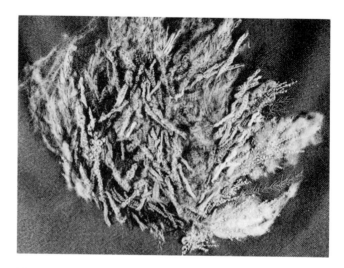

Fig. 10.13 Detail of *Emerging Spring*.

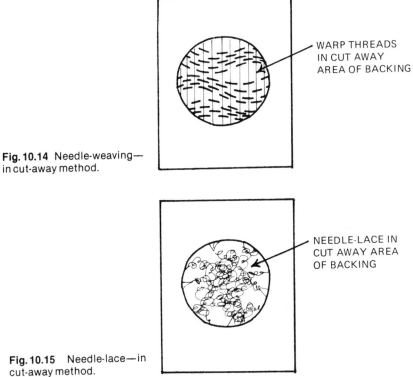

WARP THREADS
IN CUT AWAY
AREA OF BACKING

Fig. 10.14 Needle-weaving—
in cut-away method.

NEEDLE-LACE IN
CUT AWAY AREA
OF BACKING

Fig. 10.15 Needle-lace—in
cut-away method.

warp threads are laid in. When the weaving is finished, bring the thread through to the wrong side, secure with a back stitch or two, and clip off.

In loosely woven background materials such as burlap or monk's cloth, threads can be withdrawn from the cloth, leaving open areas and exposed warp threads upon which to weave or work the buttonhole stitch or any other suitable stitch you might like to try.

Another idea is to cut away sections of fabric from a backing and laying in warp threads in the negative space which can then be woven. This same idea also can be worked out using needle-lace to fill the negative space, securing the first few stitches to the cut edges and attaching it where desired on those cut edges (see Figs. 10.14 and 10.15). Allow your imagination full rein to explore the possibilities inherent in needle-weaving. Making a series of small trial pieces or working out several different approaches on a sample piece is a good way to record your explorations.

BASKETRY TECHNIQUES ADAPTABLE TO TEXTILES

Some of the techniques used in making baskets are very applicable for use in textile constructions. Of particular personal interest, coiling has been found

Fig. 10.16 Coiled wall-piece with braids (author).

to be versatile and adaptable to the creation of free, unstructured pieces. Coiling works up quite nicely if heavy yarns and twines are used. Watching a piece grow, its shape bending to the manipulations of your fingers, is fascinating and very absorbing.

Coiling is the process of winding or wrapping a thread, yarn, string, etc., around a stout cord or twine, fashioning the wrapped twine into coils and securing the coils in place with a basketry stitch. The cord or twine being wrapped is called the core. The core is what gives substance to the form being developed. The materials used for wrapping the core can range from strings, yarns, raffia, or wire to silken threads and perle cotton. The heavier

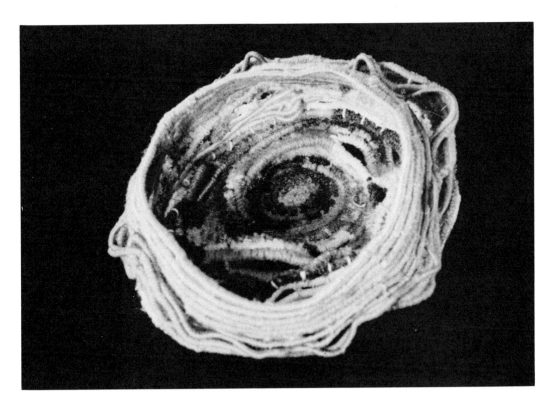

Fig. 10.17 Coiled container (author).

the wrapping medium, the faster the work progresses. Wrapping a core with fine thread can be a life's work!

When beginning to coil, thread a sturdy, blunt-pointed needle with about 36 inches of the wrapping yarn. Using the loose end (not the needle end), wind the yarn around the core about 2 inches from the core end. If you are using a heavy twine for a core, taper the end of it by trimming it to a point with scissors to insure a smooth junction blend at the beginning coil. Overlap the first wind to prevent slipping. When you wind to about ½ inch from the tapered end, bend the core back on itself to form a loop, then wind in the tapered end, always wrapping snugly. Insert the needle in the center of the wrapped loop, forming a coil, and continue wrapping from front to back; the coils are attached to each other as they are made (see Fig. 10.18).

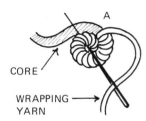

CORE

WRAPPING →
YARN

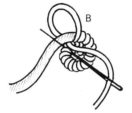

Fig. 10.18 Coiling—basic technique.

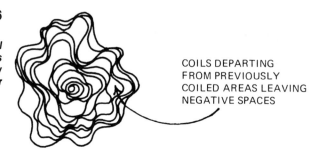

COILS DEPARTING
FROM PREVIOUSLY
COILED AREAS LEAVING
NEGATIVE SPACES

Fig. 10.19 Coiling—varying the shape.

Although various basketry stitches can be used for securing the coils as they are formed, I generally use the lazy squaw and a variation of it called the lace stitch, the latter providing space between rows of coils, giving a more open appearance.

The lazy squaw stitch is done by winding the wrapping yarn from front to back, bringing the yarn from behind and over the core into the center of the coil. Pull it snugly, then continue winding and repeat the procedure where you wish to secure the newly wrapped core to the completed coil. To change the shape of the coiled object, wrap it at uneven intervals, allowing parts of the wrapped core to extend beyond the previously coiled edges (see Fig. 10.19), then secure with the lazy squaw stitch. Much variation in shaping is

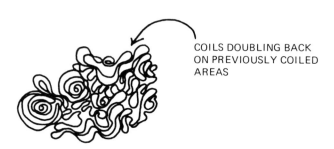

COILS DOUBLING BACK
ON PREVIOUSLY COILED
AREAS

Fig. 10.20 Coiling—doubling back technique.

easily done by irregular spacing of the wrapped core. One can double back on completed sections or attach new coils wherever fancy dictates to get a very abstract shaping (see Fig. 10.20). Of course, one can also work very symmetrically and traditionally if that is one's bent. The technique is so malleable that whatever the artist's design thrust the coils can reflect it.

The variation on the lazy squaw stitch, called the lace stitch, is done by knotting the lazy squaw stitch before continuing on with the winding. When the long stitch of the lazy squaw is made over the core, bring the wrapping yarn *over* that long stitch from the left and *under* it from the right, forming a knot; continue wrapping the core until the next stitch is desired. Pull up the knots snugly. If more space is wished between the coils, double the knot by repeating the wrapping procedure over the long stitch of the lazy squaw stitch twice. As the motion becomes familiar—and it will!—it becomes almost automatic; chances are you can devise your own variations for securing the coils. The important point to remember is that these coils can be manipulated as you see fit—they do not have to be even, symmetrical, or structured in any way unless you want them to be.

Yarns, wire, string, leather strips, plastic—whatever can be wrapped, are possibilities to use in coiling. Odd materials sometimes look extremely dramatic when used to wind onto cores. Avoid easily broken threads or those which shed. I tried wrapping with a chenille yarn which had a lovely texture but, alas, after about three winds all the chenille fibers shredded from the thread and I was left holding the denuded filament. Wrapping yarns can be interchanged at will by cutting off the end of the yarn being used, rethreading the needle with another yarn, laying the cut edge of the discarded yarn lengthwise along the core, and including it as you begin winding on the new yarn. As you resume winding with the new yarn, lay an inch or so of it along the core with the cut edge of the old yarn, both ends facing the direction toward which you are winding. Wind toward the cut ends, covering them with the new winding making a neat, tight wrap with no wisps showing. Although reading about the method might sound a bit puzzling, once it is tried the pieces of the puzzle fall into place and it generally becomes clear—indeed so undemanding that full concentration can then be put into the shape being formed and the colors being used.

To end a coiled piece taper the core and lay a sturdy needle along the core to include it in the winding which should be very tight. When you've wound the core the length of the included needle, withdraw it, and push the threaded needle opposite the direction of the winding into the space vacated by the now-removed other needle. Pull the threaded needle out of the winding, clipping the protruding end of the yarn flush to the wound core. For extra security against the cut end slipping and then unraveling, put a speck of white glue on that place and also at the tapered end of the core which is covered by winds. It's a bit tricky to end a coiled piece neatly, just as it is to begin one tidily. However, with experience one tends to become pretty deft in handling these situations.

Another method of forming handsome basket forms in fiber is by crochet which is fast and can be traditional or abstract in approach. By simply using crochet with rope, jute, twine, sturdy weaving yarns, and similar stout materials unusual forms can be made; one can add or substract the crochet stitches to make the form develop as wished. One can also combine coiling with crochet in a single piece if the design would be enhanced by such a mixture.

Experiment by making these forms so the procedure will be familiar if the occasion arises for their use. Besides, they are really therapeutic and relaxing methods for most people who enjoy working with their hands. Perhaps that is why many hospitals include this kind of hand work in their therapy sessions for the troubled.

FREE EMBROIDERY ON CANVAS

The use of randomly placed straight stitches on canvas is a departure from the usual, which is carefully structured stitches placed on a canvas background. In placement very much like that described in needle-weaving, straight stitches are criss-crossed on the canvas, building up the surface layer by layer in an abstract approach, stressing color interaction while covering the canvas backing (see Fig. 10.21). Use color carefully, placing the darks

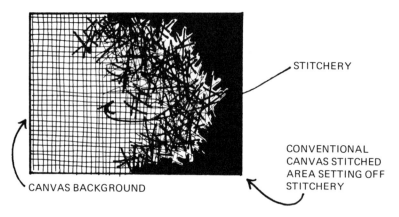

STITCHERY

CONVENTIONAL
CANVAS STITCHED
AREA SETTING OFF
STITCHERY

CANVAS BACKGROUND

Fig. 10.21 Embroidery on canvas.

and lights to form a pleasing design focus. Step a few feet away from the work and analyze what is happening to the colors from a distance. It is easier to check the color blocks by standing away from the work than it is when working closely to it; adjust any color weaknesses by placement of additional straight stitches. Experimenting with color by developing this kind of a surface is absorbing and sometimes surprising as one discovers what tricks the eye can play when colors are positioned next to each other. The pointillism used by the French painter, Seurat—the placing of small dots of various colors beside each other, allowing the eye to mix them—is an example of this type of colorplay.

Surfaces of this kind can be created on backgrounds other than canvas, of course, but the firmness of canvas is sometimes a desirable factor when working out some design ideas. And, too, the abstract part of your design on the canvas can be set off by surrounding it with solid color worked in a conventional canvas stitch.

"SCRAP" LACE

A most interesting variety of "lace," which I've labelled scrap lace for want of a better term, was observed at an arts and crafts fair which featured, in addition to the contemporary crafts, a selection of antique crafts. Among the quilts, samplers, afghans, and doilies was a lacelike swatch about 12 inches long and 4 inches wide which was carefully spread out on the upholstered arm of an antique settee.

The lacy piece was composed of tiny scraps of printed cotton fabrics cut in vaguely floral shapes, edged with buttonhole stitch in white thread, each small segment attached to its components with long bars, made by buttonholing over long connecting stitches (see Fig 10.22). The work was meticulously done and adroitly put together to form a most charming overall pattern. This type of lace development was new to me and piqued my interest to the extent of trying to make a piece of it. It is not a technique for those who are in a hurry as it works up very slowly, but the effect is unique and was, to me, worth the effort. If you wish to try it, cut shapes of cloth in any way pleasing to you, work the buttonhole stitch around the shapes, then attach them to each other by long stitches, buttonholing along the long connecting stitches to form bars. This could be tried using yarn instead of thread for the buttonholing and large pieces of fabric which would work up

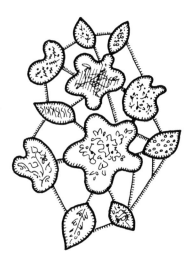

Fig. 10.22 Scrap lace.

much faster although the same method would be used. There was such an air of old-world charm in the original piece I saw, the prints faded, the thread yellowed with age, that unless one worked with old thread and fabrics it would be difficult to duplicate the aura of that fragment of yesterday. However, the method itself is adaptable to several interpretations and is a nifty way to use up scraps of cloth too small for much of anything else. It's fun, too, to let the piece develop as you work on it and to see what the end result will be like.

Old methods are continually being rediscovered and interpreted to complement today's designing.

SHISHA MIRRORS

The magical sparkle of shisha mirrors—as seen in Pakistani and Indian embroidery—is very often seen in contemporary stitchery, functional and non-functional. There are many methods of "caging" the mirrors—securing them in a border of stitchery—with directions for those ways most commonly used easily found in many contemporary stitchery books. A less structured way of attaching the mirrors and which gives a more spontaneous look to a piece, is by criss-crossing straight stitches over the mirror, varying the length of the stitches (see Fig. 10.23). The stitches can be left simply as straight stitches or they can be buttonholed for greater substance, the slight twist that is obtained by buttonholing giving a rather unusual look. You can also attach another contrasting thread after laying in the straight stitches and, with the new thread, wrap each straight stitch, beginning from the central junction of the stitches, continuing outward for just a few wraps so the mirror is not covered. This adds a nice little center interest to the covering stitches. If you lay in an uneven number of straight stitches they can be woven, under and over successive stitches, beginning from the central

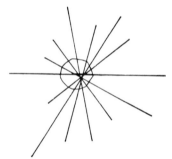

Fig. 10.23 Straight-stitch method of attaching Shisha mirrors.

junction, weaving outward for a woven center interest. The straight stitches are most attractive if they appear accidental—almost as if the mirror had dropped on the cloth and a spider had decided to encase it within its web. You might like to try this way of using mirrors.

CROCHETED HELIXES

To make a long curled strand of crocheting begin with a line of chain stitches. Then single crochet into each chain stitch once, twice, or three times. A gentle twist will result from crocheting only once in the chain stitch, with the twist getting curlier if you increase the number of stitches piled into it. Usually three is about all that will fit into the space. The helix will shorten considerably as it twists, so allow for this when chaining the foundation strand (see Fig. 10.24). If a wider helix is wished, crochet another row using the same number of stitches as are in the previous row or, for a slightly different look, increase once or more in each stitch of that row. Try a few helixes using each variation to compare the appearance of each.

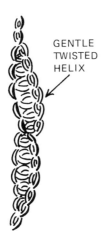

GENTLE
TWISTED
HELIX

Fig. 10.24 Crocheted helix.

OTHER CROCHET POSSIBILITIES

Combining a crocheted mesh with weaving is a variation you might like to try. To make an experimental swatch, crochet a line of chain stitches about ten inches long. Single crochet in the first row. Then in the succeeding rows, triple crochet in a stitch, skip two or three stitches, then triple crochet again and so on, developing a mesh into which one can weave any materials one fancies—such as yarns, rags, plastic, or twine. The mesh serves as the warp into which the weft (the term denoting the medium with which one weaves) is woven (see Fig. 10.25).

Crocheting over a core, such as a heavy twine, is a way of establishing a very sturdy surface, sculptural in feeling. The core gives added body to the crochet and enables one to crochet with a fine yarn and still get a robust

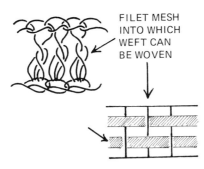

FILET MESH
INTO WHICH
WEFT CAN
BE WOVEN

Fig. 10.25 Crocheted mesh for weaving.

surface because of the firmness of the inner core. This is a method used in crocheting rugs but one which can very easily be adapted for use in hangings and soft sculpture.

WORKING WITH FELT

Felt lends itself to many fascinating manipulations. It is easy to work with, having a minimum of built-in frustrating qualities because of its nonraveling factor. It can be folded, gathered, pleated, crumpled, twisted, stuffed, quilted, combined with other techniques, and can be cut in ways to produce relief surfaces. It is suitable for appliqué and soft sculpture as well as for stitchery. It is well worthwhile to gather together a selection of felts to try various ways of surface distortion, exploring all the possibilities one can think of in using felt. A piece made while experimenting with cutting and folding felt, contrasted a folded, horizontal linear section with another horizontal plane with cut folds which provided a good textural differential to the folded area. The experiment was finally turned into a wall hanging, by the addition of crochet, stitchery, and hooking.

The best way to learn about the qualities of felt and other materials is to make small experimental studies—analogous to the sketches a graphic artist makes—each study concentrating on a specific aspect of the material, whether it be folding, crushing, gathering, or whatever.

Investigate hitherto unknown techniques to find out if and how they fit into your design direction. The addition of once unfamiliar processes to one's storehouse of information is good insurance against going stale in the pursuit of creative expression.

11 Summing Up

Although fiber as a medium for creative expression has gained increasingly wider acceptance in the art world, many artist/craftspeople have yet to explore its possibilities. It is hoped—and there seems to be good reason to believe—that the growing numbers of fiber exhibitions with their attendant publicity, coupled with the plethora of books and periodicals dealing with the subject, will trigger a wave of enthusiasm for things fibrous; that more people will experiment with this fascinating medium. New materials as well as new ways of using old materials make the field of fiber art a continually evolving creative adventure.

Clearly the ways in which people approach the resolution of design problems are as varied as are the results. Tastes, work methods, materials usage, and design attack are matters of opinion with few if any hard and fast rules. Some of the conclusions I have reached may provoke lively disagreement; good! A bland acceptance of someone else's artistic ruminations is like staying within the lines in a coloring book. However, there are a few observations I'd like to make in this chapter for your consideration, agreement, or rejection, but which might, in any case, stimulate some thought.

Too frequently we are bombarded with massiveness in fiber shows. It is unfortunate that the size of a piece is often a factor in determining its worth. If a work is executed on a grand scale, its monumental aspect alone is all too often considered to be sufficient reason to equate it with validity in the eyes of many viewers who allow their artistic judgment to be clouded in the face of impressive size. Some rather dull design ideas resolved on a huge scale are thus given undeserved acclaim, while smaller, much more innovative pieces are passed by unnoticed. It would be a refreshing change if exhibition organizers would welcome with equal warmth entries of any size—subjecting all to the same criteria for acceptance. Many artists feel pressured into working beyond their natural scale simply to get their works accepted for showing. Of course there are some exhibitions with basic ground rules which deliberately limit the specifications for entries. This is acceptable because the entrants know in advance what the conditions are for exhibiting. A good example of this kind of exhibition was one called "The First International Exhibition of Miniature Textiles," held at the British Crafts Centre, London, England, in November 1974. The size limitation set by the organizers was 8 square inches in area. An excellent article called "Fiber Works in Miniature," by Jack Lenor Larsen in *Crafts Horizons*, February 1975, discusses this exhibition and the philosophy which generated its organization. In the exhibition catalog, Revel Oddy (a member of the BCC's International Committee and Keeper of Art and Archeology at the Royal Scottish Museum in Edinburgh) writes: "The exhibition has been organized as a result of a growing feeling, in some cases conviction, that size may often take the place of quality . . . the concept of the exhibition . . . immediately raises the much debated subject of the relationship between art and size." Perhaps fiber exhibitions such as this one will lessen the reliance by some artists on massive size to gain recognition and acceptance of their works.

Among artists of any kind, there are many levels of development and many degrees of commitment in the pursuit of their art. Ideally there should be enjoyment and satisfaction in one's work at whatever level one is working whether beginning, intermediate, or advanced master. While most creative people find the continuing artistic search stimulating and challenging, their pleasure in their current level of expertise generally remains constant, even allowing for those occasional periods of discouragement. Similarly, the feelings of satisfaction enjoyed are strong whether one is committed to working as a full-time artist or as one who uses his or her creativity as a relaxing avocation, consuming only a portion of one's working or leisure hours. To the less-than-full-time person who nonetheless takes creative expression seriously, any suggestion of it as a "hobby" is anathema. The word itself conjures up visions of the hackneyed designed of kits (kitsch?) with their preplanned color schemes, the "cuteness" of the majority of crafts as offered by newsstand crafts magazines, and the commonplace yarns supplied in most of these dreary projects. Reading the books and magazines presenting fiber art on an equal footing with other visual arts keeps one knowledgeable about current developments in the fiber art world (as well as in the other arts) and helps stamp out possible tendencies toward triviality in one's work. It is well to maintain an open but critical, flexible but questioning mind, which considers new ideas and directions, accepting and rejecting with thought and perception. Controversy arising from unconventional use of materials, colors, or designs, while leaving oneself vulnerable to unfavorable criticism, is nevertheless not to be avoided. Nothing new would then ever be tried!

Along with keeping an active, open, and questioning mind, it is well to grow in consciousness of what is beautiful in living. The search for beauty should not be confined to the overwhelming experiences; the humble and simple elements of one's everyday surroundings often make the greatest impact if we have the sensitivity to recognize their intrinsic beauty. The book, *Forms in Japan*, by Yiuchiro Kojiro, illustrates this point tellingly with striking photographs of the forms we see all the time—the rocks in a garden, the textures of our natural and man-made environment, the tools we use and take for granted, the shapes and rhythm of waves in motion, and so much more. Listen to the sound of rain, the rustle of wind-blown grasses, the night creatures' orchestrations; smell the fragrance of sun-dried clothes, fresh-cut grass. We are enveloped by the lovely web of life—we have only to look, to touch, to smell, to listen. Perhaps the meaning of life is only being. But that is for philosophers to ponder. . . .

One of the nicest aspects of fiber art is that much can be done with little, and one can engage in the field with small expenditure. Materials can be as simple as hardware store twine, recycled fabrics, and minimum amounts of threads and yarns. Of course one *can* spend a great deal on the finest textiles, silk threads, hand-spun yarns, and the like. But the point remains that one *needn't*! Use imagination and ingenuity in materials selection and think twice about throwing anything away. Become acquainted with your friendly neighborhood thrift shop for all sorts of fascinating stuff, and don't neglect the flea markets and rummage sales.

It is interesting, after having been involved in fiber art for a time, to look back and see how one's tastes have changed as experience and knowledge have increased. Reviewing pieces done in the beginning period and contrasting them with current work generally points up the sometimes drastic changes which have occurred in aesthetic judgment over the time span. Sometimes an old idea redone in light of present judgment is a good exercise to demonstrate how far you have traveled. Often, it will be rather surprising to realize how color ideas have evolved and how naive old color preferences now seem. With experience, continual observation, and learning, color concepts usually become much more sophisticated and subtle as do design resolutions. The probability of choosing the obvious solution to a design problem is minimized with heightened perception.

With this increasing aesthetic perception comes concomitant appreciation of the value of simplicity. Many beginners tend to overwork their pieces, using too many colors and too much stitch variety in a single design, resulting in busy, fussy work. As knowledge and experience increase, however, a gradual process of elimination usually takes place in the

Fig. 11.1 Wall-piece crocheted with sewing thread, mounted on recycled wire—materials costing next to nothing (author).

execution of work. The number of colors in a design are limited; more attention is paid to the overall concept with less emphasis given to each individual component. A more cohesive result is achieved. "Make more of less," a saying attributed to Buckminster Fuller, sums up a desirable direction in which to go—and not only in art!

Simple is beautiful—an idea well illustrated by works of many cultures; I think particularly of the Scandinavians and the Japanese who seem to have mastered in their art a purity of line and form enchanting to the eye. The magazine *Embroidery*, Winter 1975, offers a brief but telling article about May Morris, an English embroiderer and teacher. Miss Morris, in a listing of preparatory notes for classroom instruction, makes this observation: "You must also make your spaces interesting—for restraint tells us as much as profusion—more."

Just as reduction of overelaboration in work comes with an educated taste, so too does the concept of process being of greater importance than product. In the actual *doing*, the greater satisfaction comes. The end product is rewarding, of course, but we experience pleasure primarily by process—including the process of learning. Process need not be an individual endeavor. Group projects involve the interaction of fellow craftspeople, all engaged in the creation of something of common interest. This type of cooperative venture of like-minded colleagues can be fulfilling and rewarding in ways that individual projects never can. The exchange of ideas and expertise is brainstorming on-the-job with the added factor of lively sociability among the participants. I think of the old-time quilting bees and how pleasant they must have been and how charming the results of those group efforts often were—judging by retrospective quilt shows now so popular.

A unique group enterprise came to my attention recently. In the December 1975 issue of *Yankee* magazine, an article appeared entitled, ''Sew a Christmas.'' The article told of a large folk-art tapestry, 32 ′ × 15 ′, made by the parishioners of St. Stanislaus Polish Catholic Church in Fall River, Massachusetts. Designed by Sister Felicita Zdrojewski, an artist and designer, it was made by members of the parish who hand-appliquéd on a backing life-sized figures of a family in a traditional religious Polish Christmas setting. These dedicated church members cut and sewed together 5,293 felt pieces. For final assembly, the work was spread out on the floor of the gymnasium where dozens of sewers worked together to bring this impressive work to fruition. Hanging the tapestry in the church sanctuary during the Christmas season has become an annual tradition at St. Stanislaus Church. Visitors are welcome to view this lovely example of folk art during the holiday season. I can just imagine the joy of creation felt by all who worked on this project; how fortunate they were to have had such a special experience in their lives.

The final display or presentation of a work is vital in relation to its impact on the viewer. Just as the tapestry discussed above, hung and lighted in the church sanctuary, was shown to its fullest advantage, so should each piece be given the respect it deserves by being thoughtfully presented. Soft hang-

Fig. 11.2 *The Journey*—couched yarn with clear plastic inserts (author).

ings, unframed, should be lined—and interlined if extra body is needed. All sewing necessary for finishing should be done carefully. It is always disconcerting to see a lovely piece sloppily finished with crude sewing of linings, careless tacking onto frames, inappropriate kinds of hanging rods, and the like. Good standards of craftsmanship should prevail from beginning to end even if creative interest flags when one is down to the wire of finishing details. If a piece is to be displayed, give it a worthy setting and presentation.

It is hoped that those for whom stitchery and fiber are a new experience will find within this book some helpful ideas. For those who are already well aware of the joy of working in fiber, perhaps a few new thoughts will be gained from my observations. In any event, my hope for all who love fiber as I do is that they will go in whatever direction is most personally inspiring, enjoying long and happy lives filled with creative adventures.

Bibliography

APPLIQUÉ AND QUILTING

Laliberte, Norman, and McIlhany, Sterling. *Banners and Hangings.* New York: Van Nostrand Reinhold Co., 1966.

Laury, Jean Ray. *Appliqué Stitchery.* New York: Reinhold Book Corp., 1966.

Laury, Jean Ray. *Quilts and Coverlets.* New York: Van Nostrand Reinhold Co., 1970.

Newman, Thelma R. *Quilting, Patchwork, Appliqué and Trapunto.* New York: Crown Publishers, Inc., 1974.

Short, Eirian. *Embroidery and Fabric Collage.* New York: Charles Scribner's Sons, 1967.

Sommer, Elyse, and Sommer, Mike. *A New Look at Felt.* New York: Crown Publishers, Inc., 1975.

BASKETRY

Meilach, Dona Z. *A Modern Approach to Basketry with Fibers and Grasses.* New York: Crown Publishers, Inc., 1974.

BODY COVERINGS AND ACCESSORIES

Beagle, Peter. *American Denim.* New York: Harry N. Abrams, Inc., 1975.

Laury, Jean Ray, and Aiken, Joyce. *Creating Body Coverings.* New York: Van Nostrand Reinhold Co., 1973.

CROCHET

Dawson, Mary M. *A Complete Guide to Crochet Stitches.* New York: Crown Publishers, Inc., 1972.

MacKenzie, Clinton D. *New Design in Crochet.* New York: Van Nostrand Reinhold Co., 1972.

Sommer, Elyse, and Sommer, Mike. *A New Look at Crochet.* New York: Crown Publishers, Inc., 1975.

Ventre, Mary Tibbals. *Crochet.* Boston, Mass.: Little, Brown and Co., 1974.

DESIGN

Bates, Kenneth F. *Basic Design—Principles and Practice.* New York: Funk & Wagnalls, 1975.

Brodatz, Phil. *Textures.* New York: Dover Publications, Inc., 1966.

Chott, Orville K. *Design Is Where You Find It.* Ames, Iowa: The Iowa State University Press, 1972.

d'Arbeloff, Natalie. *Designing with Natural Forms.* New York: Watson-Guptill Publications, 1973.

deSausmarez, Maurice. *Basic Design.* New York: Van Nostrand Reinhold Co., 1964.

Itten, Johannes. *Design and Form,* rev. ed. New York: Van Nostrand Reinhold Co., 1975.

Morman, Jean Mary. *Wonder Under Your Feet.* New York: Harper & Row, Pulishers, 1973.

Munari, Bruno. *Design as Art.* Baltimore, Md.: Penguin Books, Inc., 1971.

Seyd, Mary. *Designing with String.* New York: Watson-Guptill Publications, 1967.

Strache, Wolfe. *Forms and Patterns in Nature.* New York: Pantheon Books, Random House, 1973.

Waller, Irene. *Designing with Threads.* New York: Viking Press. 1973.

GENERAL

Bakke, Karen. *The Sewing Machine as a Creative Tool.* Englewood Cliffs, N.J.: Prentice-Hall, Inc., 1976.

Birrell, Verla. *The Textile Arts.* New York: Harper & Row, Publishers, 1959.

Feininger, Andreas. *Roots of Art.* New York: Viking Press, 1975.

Kojiro, Yuichiro. *Forms in Japan.* Honolulu: East-West Center Press, 1963.

Mante, Harold. *Color Design in Photography.* New York: Van Nostrand Reinhold Co., 1972.

Paz, Octavio. *In Praise of Hands.* Greenwich, Conn.: Graphic Society, 1974.

Stribling, Mary Lou. *Crafts from North American Indian Art.* New York: Crown Publishers, Inc., 1975.

KNITTING

Cone, Ferne Geller. *Knit Art.* New York: Van Nostrand Co., 1975.

Phillips, Mary Walker. *Creative Knitting.* New York: Van Nostrand Reinhold Co., 1971.

LACE

Nordfors, Jill. *Needle Lace and Needleweaving.* New York: Van Nostrand Reinhold Co., 1974.

Pfannschmidt, Ernst-Erik. *Twentieth-Century Lace.* New York: Charles Scribner's Sons, 1975.

MACRAMÉ

Harvey, Virginia I. *Color and Design in Macramé.* New York: Van Nostrand Reinhold Co., n.d.

Meilach, Dona Z. *Macramé—Creative Design in Knotting.* New York: Crown Publishers, Inc., 1971.

SOFT SCULPTURE AND TEXTILE CONSTRUCTIONS

Constantine, Mildred, and Larsen, Jack Lenor. *Beyond Craft: The Art Fiber.* New York: Van Nostrand Reinhold Co., 1973.

Fisch, Arline M. *Textile Techniques in Metal.* New York: Van Nostrand Reinhold Co., 1975.

Frew, Hannah. *Three-Dimensional Embroidery.* New York: Van Nostrand Reinhold Co., 1975.

Hutton, Helen. *Textile Structures.* New York: Watson-Guptill Publications, 1975.

Meilach, Dona Z. *Soft Sculpture and Other Soft Art Forms.* New York: Crown Publishers, Inc., 1974.

Meilach, Dona Z., and Ten Hoor, Elvie. *Collage and Assemblage.* New York: Crown Publishers, Inc., 1973.

Stribing, Mary Lou. *Art from Found Materials.* New York: Crown Publishers, Inc., 1970.

STITCHERY

deDillmont, Th. *The Complete Encyclopedia of Needlework.* Philadelphia, Pa.: Running Press, 1972.

Enthoven, Jacqueline. *The Stitches of Creative Embroidery.* New York: Reinhold Book Corp., 1968.

Howard, Constance. *Inspiration for Embroidery.* Newton Centre, Mass.: Charles T. Branford Co., 1967.

Karasz, Mariska. *Adventures in Stitches.* New York: Funk & Wagnalls, 1959.

Krevitsky, Nik. *Stitchery: Art and Craft.* New York: Reinhold Book Corp., 1969.

143

Bibliography

Rush, Beverly. *The Stitchery Idea Book.* New York: Van Nostrand Reinhold Co., 1974.

Snook, Barbara. *Needlework Stitches.* New York: Crown Publishers, Inc., 1963.

Willcox, Donald J. *New Design in Stitchery.* New York: Van Nostrand Reinhold, 1970.

PUBLICATIONS

Crafts. Crafts Advisory Committee, 12 Waterloo Place, London SW1Y 4AU, England.

Crafts Horizons. American Crafts Council, 44 West 53rd Street, New York, N.Y. 10019.

Embroidery. The Embroiderers' Guild, 73 Wimpole Street, London W1M 8AX, England.

Fiberarts Magazine. Fiberarts Magazine, 3717 4th Street N.W., Albuquerque, New Mexico 87107.

Shuttle, Spindle & Dyepot. Handweavers Guild of America, Inc., 998 Farmington Ave., West Hartford, Connecticut 06107.

Index